Best Friends
forever!

Photography by Louis Wallach
Additional photographs by Anthony Lowe, Dietrich Gehring, and Chuck Solomon

Illustrated instructions by Elara Tanguy

Design and Art Direction by Janet Parker

Library of Congress Cataloging-in-Publication Data

Torres, Laura
  Best friends forever! : 199 projects to make and share / by Laura Torres.
    p. cm
  ISBN 0-7611-3274-0 (alk. paper)
    1. Handicraft for girls—Juvenile literature. I. Title

TT171.T6697 2004
745.5—dc22

2004045635

Workman books are available at special discounts when purchased in bulk for premiums
and sales promotions as well as for fund-raising or educational use.
Special editions or book excerpts can also be created to specification.
For details, contact the Special Sales Director at the address below.

Workman Publishing Company, Inc.
708 Broadway
New York, NY 10003-9555
www.workman.com

Printed in the United States of America

First printing June 2004

10 9 8 7 6 5 4 3 2 1

Best Friends
forever!
199 projects to make and share

BY LAURA TORRES

WORKMAN PUBLISHING, NEW YORK

Contents

Shadowbox Photo Tin, page 8

Dizzy Notes,
page 24

Jellied Bubbles,
page 44

Footnotes, page 76

top: Pajama Pant Swap, page 96

Friendly Fun & Games 115

Two-of-a-Kind Jewelry 133

Friendship
Stack Rings,
page 134

Fun Things to
Do with School
Photos, page 128

Introduction

Nothing is as much fun as making things to share with good friends, especially your BFF (Best Friend Forever). Together, you can create two-of-a-kind crafts that will express your friendship and your creative spirit. But even *better* is the time you will spend together planning and creating great things to use, wear, and share. A friendship with a DIY (Do-It-Yourself) attitude is a friendship full of creative possibilities—there is always something to do.

My BFF, Pam, and I started crafting together the first time I went over to her house. We spent hours making wild creatures out of a couple of pairs of old toe socks. When we were done, she gave her *best* one to me, and I gave mine to her. A BFF friendship was born.

After that, we made everything together, from lip gloss and nylon dolls to a bizarre, rattling go-cart that was hard to steer. To Pam and me, there was nothing like the feeling of flying down a hill in a go-cart we made ourselves, or wearing matching bracelets we made for each other. We were, and still are, Do-It-Yourself girls, and proud of it.

I'm sharing my *best* friendship crafts and activities in this *book* for you and all your friends. You should be able to find most of the materials you need around the house, or at discount and thrift stores. All are easy and inexpensive to make, but most of all, they are symbols of your one-of-a-kind friendship. And if you decide to make a go-cart

(instructions NOT included), remember to proudly wear your crash helmets. So grab your BFF and go make something!

Where to Find Stuff

Craft stores, of course, are the obvious places to find most craft supplies. Sometimes, though, they carry the same old predictable stuff, so shopping there can be downright uninspiring. I like dollar stores, drug stores, Wal-Mart–like department stores, hardware stores (where you can find great glues, tapes, and heavy-duty magnets), secondhand stores, flea markets, and garage sales.

You can often find one-of-a-kind things that are begging to be made into something else. That too-gaudy dollar necklace? Maybe you can take it apart and use the antique beads for

Paper Flowers, page 53

a matching pair of earrings for you and your friend. I once bought one old sweater for $2 and used it to make four matching handbags for myself and three friends. The collar of the sweater had some interesting beads sewn on; I pulled them off and used them to decorate the purses so each one was a little different.

Better yet, look in your own drawers and closets (and in the drawers and closets of anyone else who will let you). Free is always best! A pair of socks with stretched-out elastic? Sock Bunnies waiting to happen. Leftover tissue paper from a birthday party? Throw it in your supply box to use later to make a Pop Vase. And when you're friendship crafting, always be on the lookout for anything that comes in twos. Happy hunting!

The Secrets of Sticking

Most craft books will tell you to use glue when sticking paper together. When it's possible, I say always use double-sided tape. Why? Because if you've ever tried to glue one piece of paper neatly to another, you know it's almost impossible to avoid the dreaded glue bumps. Double-sided tape is a must-have for easy, clean sticking.

When you must use glue, forget that thin white glue, and instead use a thick white craft glue like Sobo. Googly eyes stay put and won't slide around, and it works on fibers like felt, denim, and yarn without soaking through and getting all funky.

For anything that needs some heavy-duty staying power, you need a strong glue like E-6000 or Plumber's Goop. They smell bad and you'll need some parental help, but these inconveniences are worth the sticking power. Superglue might do if you don't have anything else, but I like the thickness of the other glues.

Basic Sewing

A regular straight stitch (in and out) is right for most sewing projects. Here's the easiest way: Double the thread on the needle. Tie a knot at the end with both pieces. This will keep your needle from sliding off.

Sew a row of stitches in and out, like this:

Tie a knot at the end, but don't forget this trick: Pull the thread tight *sloooowly*. This will prevent the knot from going tight too early and leaving you with a bunch of tangled-up loops.

Loop thread around needle twice.

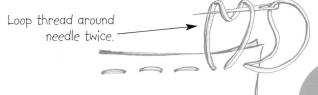

ix

My Craft Closet

*Y*ou don't have to have a room-size closet like mine—stuffed full of pipe cleaners and pom-poms and cool candy wrappers and 14,000 *skeins* of embroidery floss and boxes and boxes of things that I *know* I'll use in a project someday. There are a few things, however, that you should stock up on to make some of the crafts in this book. A good Do-It-Yourself team always keeps its eye out for a bargain or a hidden treasure at a garage sale or thrift store. If you share supplies with

a friend, you'll have more variety and you can make things cheaper. One big box ought to do it for you and a friend.

You can probably find the stuff on this side around the house or secondhand.

Bottles

Empty candy tins

Matchboxes

Socks, mismatched or otherwise

Interesting beads & buttons

Old jeans, shirts & sweaters with great pockets or sleeves

Plain picture frames

Interesting charms

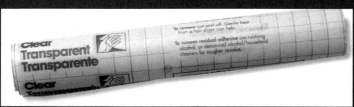
Clear contact paper

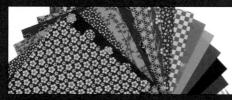
Glitter glue

Dimensional paint (any kind in a *squeeze* bottle, such as fabric paints)

Origami or scrapbook paper

On this side are the things I can't craft without. You might want to pick these up when you see them on sale.

Alphabet beads

Wire in different gauges

Double-stick tape

Craft floss or embroidery floss

Mod Podge

Thick, white craft glue (My favorite is Sobo craft and fabric glue.)

E-6000 glue or Plumber's Goop (very sticky, thick, and strong)

Make Friends, Make Crafts

A good friend is like a four-leaf clover: hard to find and lucky to have. So if you have a BFF, you are a lucky girl. If you have more than one BFF, you are extra-lucky! Friendship is all about fun and caring and being together, so the more BFFs you have, the better.

Question: What's the best vitamin for making friends?

Answer: B-1

Corny, but true. There are a lot of activities in this book you can do to become a better friend, and many you can use to make new friends.

Is there a new girl in school who eats lunch at your table? Make her a braided friendship bracelet to make her feel welcome. Maybe you are the new kid at school—make bracelets for the girls who invited you to sit with them. Does a girl at your church draw amazing doodles? Ask her to draw something for a Picture Clippy and then make one for her, too. There are many ways you can be a good friend, some as simple as smiling and saying "Hi," and some as super as inviting someone to make Fuzzy Dudes with you.

I keep a card on my bulletin board that says, "Friends are the sunshine of life." Get out there and spread some rays!

—❤ Laura

Say Cheese!

photo fun

*how to take a great

When you're taking a picture, tuck your arms tight against your body. This will help with the wobbles that can cause a blurry shot.

If you take a photo outside, don't shoot into the sun, and don't put your friend in the sun— she'll look all squinty. Have her stand in the shade. If you take the photo inside, use a flash.

picture of your friend

Pay attention to the background. You don't want your friend to look like she has a lamppost or tree growing out of her head.

Close-up shots are better. Who needs a ton of background when the star is your friend?

To get a more natural shot, have your friend lean in toward you. Also, if she's got a stiff smile, she'll look more natural if you have her look away for a moment, while you tell her your funniest joke, then have her look back at the camera. Shoot quick! Use lots of film, so you have lots to choose from.

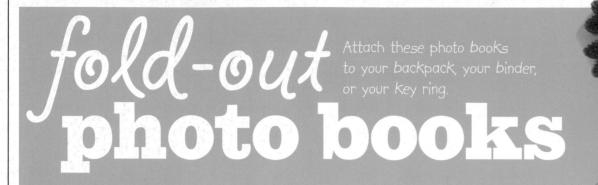

fold-out photo books

Attach these photo books to your backpack, your binder, or your key ring.

You will need:

Craft foam

Ruler

A pencil

Paper

Scissors

Pictures of you and your friends

Tape

Double-stick tape

Velcro sticky dots

A small hole punch

A ball chain

6.5 inches

1.5 inches

.5 inch

1.75 inches

Velcro dot

Velcro dot (on back)

1 Using a ruler, draw this pattern on paper following the measurements shown. Cut it out.

2 Trace around the pattern you just made on the craft foam and cut it out.

3 Fold the foam at the dotted lines. Stick a Velcro sticky dot on the tab and the back of the book.

4 Cut an initial or other shapes out of craft foam and decorate the front of the book. Double-stick tape works well.

5 Photocopy your pictures so they are all about the same size. Tape them together in strips and fan-fold between the photos.

6 Use double-stick tape to attach the first picture inside the booklet. Fold up the pictures and fasten the book closed.

7 Punch a hole in the corner of the book. Thread a ball chain through the hole.

back of photo

back of photo

.....back.....

tape

tape

fantastic frames

You and your friend will look smashing in matching fluffy picture frames. One time Pam and I decided we were going to do a photo shoot as if we were models. We tried a little too hard, and the results were stiff and scary (too much makeup!). Natural shots are best.

You will need:

Picture frames

Photos

A boa, pom-poms, or bead trim and glitter

Thick white craft glue

1 Cut the boa or trim to fit around the frame. If your boa or trim frays easily, put a little glue on the cut ends.

2 Squeeze plenty of glue around frame. Carefully stick on the boa or trim, pressing it into the glue as you go. Let dry. Add another layer of trim, some glitter, or whatever else you want.

3 Add your photos, you gorgeous things, you!

I like black-and-white photos in bright frames. Try shooting a roll of black-and-white film or photocopy a color print in black and white. —❤ *Laura*

Where do you find old picture frames, trims, and boas? At the dollar store, the craft store, big discount stores like Wal-Mart (look in the craft section for boas), and thrift stores. Check out the trim section of the fabric store for cheap, fun stuff such as rick-rack, pom-poms, and beaded trims.

The picture frames you find can be ugly, because you're going to cover them up anyway. I picked up some usable green frames with pictures of ducks in them for a dime each at a garage sale. I took out the quackers and glued rick-rack and beads to the frames for a whole new look. If you're extra-crafty, you can make your own frames out of cardboard.

7

shadowbox photo tin

It's a shadow box! It's a picture frame! It's an empty Altoids tin! Yup, yup, and yup. Finally, something to do with all those sentimental friendship doodads you've been saving.

You will need:

An empty **Altoids tin**

Colored paper

A pencil

A photo of you and your friend

Ticket stubs, old friendship bracelets, that penguin eraser named Bob that you and your friend found at school . . . you get the idea.

Scissors

Double-stick tape

Thick, strong glue like E-6000

1 Trace around the tin two times on the colored paper. Cut out the shape, just inside the lines.

2 Use the double-stick tape to attach the paper to the insides of the tin.

3 On the shallow side, attach your picture with the double-stick tape.

4 On the deeper side, arrange your items, then glue in place with the goopy glue. Let dry.

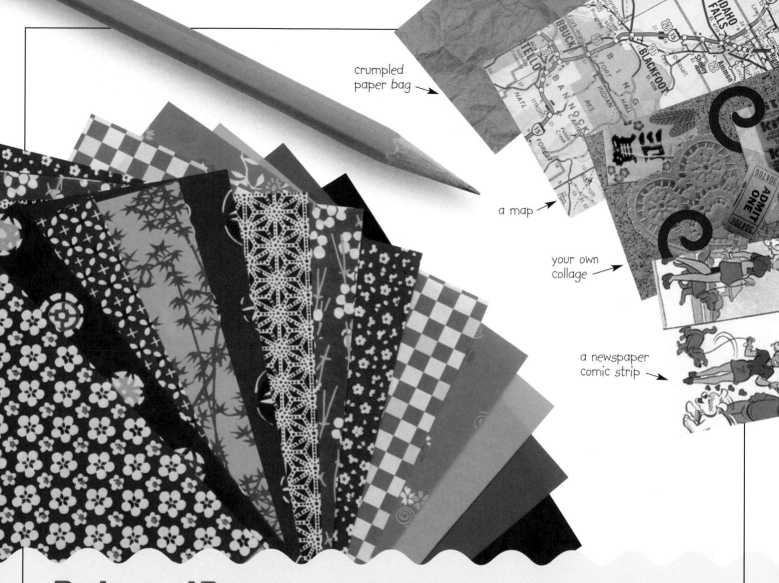

crumpled paper bag →

a map →

your own collage →

a newspaper comic strip →

Background Paper

I use a lot of origami paper in my crafting, because I love the colors and rich designs. You can also find a lot of good paper in the scrapbook section of most craft stores. If you want something more personal or handmade for your shadowbox (or any other craft), consider these ideas:

● Make a collage of letters or images from magazines. Use similar colors so it won't be too obnoxious for a background.

● Crumple up a piece of a grocery bag. Keep crumpling until it is soft. It'll look like leather and have a nice texture.

● Use a comic strip from the paper, or a section of the newspaper with the date or some timely event on it.

● Pieces of old maps make terrific background papers, especially if you can get your hands on one with a relevant location.

9

name frame

Hang up this lightweight frame anywhere—on a bulletin board, on your locker, or on your wall. Or you can even use it for the cover of a scrapbook or photo album.

You will need:

Craft foam

Scissors

Brads

A photo of you and your friend

A fine-tip permanent marker

1 Cut a piece of craft foam for the backing. It should be about 3 to 4 inches wider than your photo and about 2 inches longer. Set aside.

2 Cut two thin strips of craft foam, about ¼ inch wide. Cut out craft-foam flowers or other shapes, one for each letter in both your names.

3 Stick a brad through the center of each foam flower, then through the foam strip. On one strip, use enough flowers to spell your friend's name. On the other, use enough to spell your name.

4 Write your names on the brads with the permanent marker.

5 Cut wider craft-foam strips in a contrasting color. Glue the skinny strips with the flowers in the center of the wide strips. Lay the strips down on the backing far enough apart to hold the corners of your photo in place.

6 Glue the strips in place, but don't glue the parts where the corners of your photo will slip in. Let dry.

7 Slip in your photo. You can use some double-stick tape if you want, but it should stay put.

If your names don't fit nicely on the brads (like if your name is PJ and your friend's name is Alexandria), you can use initials or write a message instead, such as "Camp 2004" or "Best Friends" or "Say Cheese." —♥ *Laura*

11

rock stars frame

If you spend a day with your friends at the beach or at camp, collect pocketfuls of small rocks. Be sure you take a great picture—a fun close-up of all your mugs—and make this rockin' frame.

You will need:

Small rocks

A photo

A picture frame with a large, flat surface

E-6000 glue

Microbeads, small seed beads, or glitter

1 Center your photo in the frame.

2 Squeeze a thick layer of glue on a small section of the picture frame.

3 Working quickly, stick rocks in the glue.

4 Sprinkle with beads or glitter.

5 Repeat steps 2–4 until the whole frame is covered. Let dry.

12

photo flowers

School pictures need all the help they can get, so dress them up with these wire photo holders. You and your friends will look marvelous. Now if only you could do something about that photo on your Dad's driver's license . . .

You will need:

20- or 22-gauge wire

Round beads

Small pliers

Wire cutters or fingernail clippers

Small bottle or vase

1 Cut a piece of wire about 2 feet long. Use the wire cutters or fingernail clippers. (I fudge and use my scissors when I'm feeling too lazy to find the wire cutters, but it does dull the blades.)

2 Poke the end of the wire through a bead. Curl the end around the bead to hold it in place. You might need pliers to do this.

3 Twist the wire around the bead at least twice in a spiral to make the center of the flower.

4 Bend the wire to form petals around the center.

5 Bend the end of the wire straight down to make a stem.

6 Make a bunch of these flowers. Put them in a bottle or vase. Cut the ends of the wire so the flowers are at different heights and make a nice arrangement.

7 Twist all the stems together at the bottom to hold everything in place.

8 Poke your friends' pictures between the spirals of the flowers.

*scrap*bookmarks

This is one of my favorite ways to scrapbook—because it's quick, it's fun, and I can put silly hats on my friends. Plus, I love to see my friends' smiling faces when I open my *book*.

You will need:

A long, skinny **color photocopy** (or photo you can cut up) of you and your friends

Double-stick tape

Scissors

Colored paper

Stickers, old magazines, scrapbook paper, etc.

Clear contact paper

A hole punch

Craft or embroidery floss

Beads

1 Cut out the picture of you and your friends. Use double-stick tape to stick the picture to a sheet of colored paper.

2 Cut around the picture to leave a thin border of color around it. If you have a pair, use scissors that make a decorative edge.

3 Stick the whole thing to another piece of paper. Cut a wider border this time.

4 Decorate the picture with stickers, magazine cut-outs, etc.

 Before I recycle magazines, I tear out and save interesting words and pictures to use in collages later. —♥ *Laura*

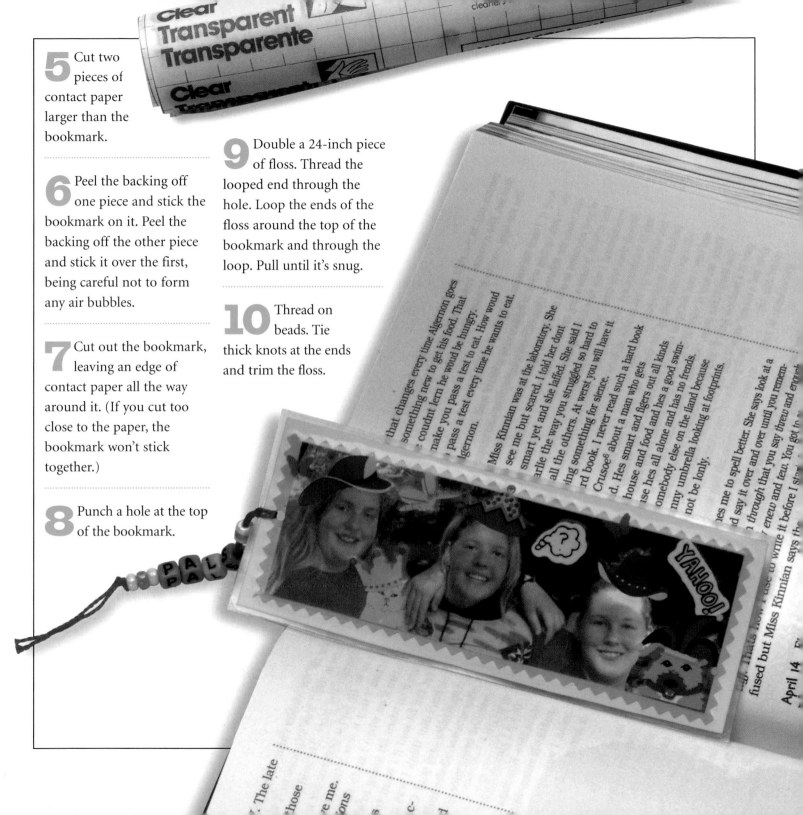

5 Cut two pieces of contact paper larger than the bookmark.

6 Peel the backing off one piece and stick the bookmark on it. Peel the backing off the other piece and stick it over the first, being careful not to form any air bubbles.

7 Cut out the bookmark, leaving an edge of contact paper all the way around it. (If you cut too close to the paper, the bookmark won't stick together.)

8 Punch a hole at the top of the bookmark.

9 Double a 24-inch piece of floss. Thread the looped end through the hole. Loop the ends of the floss around the top of the bookmark and through the loop. Pull until it's snug.

10 Thread on beads. Tie thick knots at the ends and trim the floss.

cd friends suncatcher

Even if you and your friends aren't music stars, that can't stop you from producing these original CDs. Use them to decorate your wall or locker, or hang them near a window for a star-worthy suncatcher.

You will need:

A plain CD (The ones that come in the mail for free are perfect!)

A photo

Scissors

Double-stick tape

Fabric paint

Flat-backed rhinestones (optional)

1 Cut your photo in a circle to go in the middle of the CD. Use double-stick tape to attach it.

2 Use the fabric paint to make a decorative frame around the picture and hide the cut edge.

3 Have each girl sign her name with fabric paint, and then decorate the CD. You can press flat-backed rhinestones into wet fabric paint if you want.

16

Best Friends Forever

hang it up!

Here's a cool way to hang your CD in your window to catch colorful rays. Since it will spin around, you'll want another decorated CD to glue to the back.

1 Decorate both CDs first. When they are completely dry, glue the CDs back to back, with a piece of fishing line in between.

2 Let the fishing line stick out a few inches from the bottom.

3 Thread a charm or crystal on the tail and tie it. Thread a needle on the other end of the fishing line and string on pom-poms, beads, or craft-foam shapes. Leave some space in between each, so everything seems to be floating.

4 Tie to a hook or curtain rod close to a window.

Learn from my mistake: Do not use glitter glue or white craft glue to stick anything to the CD. When the glue dries, it doesn't stick. —♥ *Laura*

17

photo box wrap

A quickie way to wrap a gift box for a friend—and the wrapping is a gift in itself. In fact, sometimes my friends have liked the box more than the gift. (Oh, well.) If you don't have an empty pop-up tissue box already, just pull all the tissues out. (Your pet will think this is great fun.) Store the tissues somewhere else.

You will need:

An empty, pretty pop-up tissue box

Scissors

A photograph

Double-stick tape

Colored paper

Ribbon

Beads, bottlecaps, rhinestones, or other embellishments

Glue

1 Cut the plastic out of the top of the box.

Cut out clear plastic.

2 Cut through three sides of the top of the box so the lid lifts open and closed.

3 Tape a photo inside the box lid so it shows through the hole in the top.

4 Tape a piece of ribbon inside the box lid so it sticks out of the front center of the lid.

Tape ribbon inside lid.

5 Cut a piece of colored paper to fit the inside of the lid. Tape in place.

6 Glue embellishments on the ribbon. If you have extra time, you can go nuts decorating the box, but it looks fine plain, too.

(Your Photo Here)

snappy shots

Get some cardboard slide mounts from a photo shop to make these small and snappy photo frames. Glue a magnet on the back for a refrigerator or locker display. Glue a few on a ribbon and hang them on your wall or set them up on your desk or dresser.

You will need:

Cardboard slide mounts

Photos

Acrylic paint or markers

Double-stick tape

Embellishments (stamp, rhinestones, ribbon, etc.)

1 Decorate the outside of the slide mount. Paint it or color it with markers. Let it dry and stamp on it or glue on embellishments.

2 Put your photo inside the slide mount. Use double-stick tape around the edges to hold the picture in place and to stick the slide mount together.

3 Now decide how to display them!

COLOR TRANSPARENCY

COLOR TRANSPARENCY

MADE IN U.S.A.

19

photo pendants

Do you have a great picture of you and your friend? Turn it into a piece of original jewelry.

You will need:

- **A small photocopy of a photo**
- **Colored paper**
- **Double-stick tape**
- **A note card**
- **Scissors**
- **Glue**
- **Beads**
- **Mod Podge** or diluted glue
- **A paintbrush**
- **24-gauge wire**

1 Cut out the photo. Use double-stick tape to attach it to colored paper.

2 Cut the paper around the photo, leaving a thin border of color.

3 Use the double-stick tape to attach the whole thing to a note card. Trim around the border.

4 Paint a coat of Mod Podge over the top of the pendant. Let dry.

5 Glue beads around the edge of pendant to make a frame. Let dry.

6 Fold an 8-inch piece of wire in half. Twist just below the fold to make a loop.

7 Thread a bead over both wire ends and push it up against the loop to hide the twist.

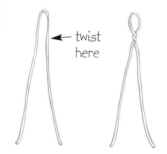

← twist here

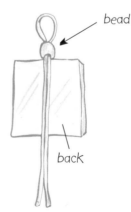

bead

back

Best Friends Forever

8 Glue the wire to the back of the pendant.

9 Cut another piece of note card to the size of the pendant. Use the double-stick tape to stick it on the back of the pendant, so the wire is sandwiched in between note-card layers. Paint a coat of Mod Podge on the back of the pendant. Let dry.

10 Thread a bead on both ends of the wire.

11 Trim the ends of the wire to about 1 inch. Curl the ends up in a spiral or separate them, twist, and add beads.

If you don't have Mod Podge, you can mix ¼ cup of Elmer's glue with ¼ cup of water. Store it in an airtight container. —♥ *Laura*

makin' copies

Color photocopies can get a bit expensive, so use this trick: Instead of copying just one photo for one project, take all the photos you like of you and your friends and tape them onto an 11- by 17-inch piece of paper. Cram on as many as you can. If you've got a lot of background you don't need in a picture, overlap another photo on top of it. Reduce this page at several different percentages. To get really tiny, reduce the page as much as you can, and then reduce the resulting photocopy. If you do it this way, you'll have lots of photos in lots of different sizes for not much money. Keep them in a file and use them for future craft projects. You'll be glad you have them.

21

photo jewelry box

These are especially for your photo pendants, of course. Use the same photo to make the box and the jewelry.

You will need:

A plain box (They come in lots of shapes and sizes for less than a dollar at the craft store.)

A photocopy of a photo

Scissors

Double-stick tape

Acrylic paint

A paintbrush

Glitter glue or dimensional paint

Glue

Glitter

Faux fur (fake fur, actually, but don't you just love the word *faux*?)

1 Paint the box and lid with the acrylic paint. Let dry.

2 Cut out the photo. Attach it to the top of the lid with double-stick tape.

3 Use glitter glue or dimensional paint to make a frame around the photo. Press in some beads if you want. Let dry.

4 Paint a coat of glue on the rest of the lid. Sprinkle with glitter. Tap off the excess.

5 Trace around the bottom of the box on the wrong side of the faux fur. Cut out.

6 Glue fur inside the bottom of the box.

Pass It On!
cool notes

dizzy notes

Write a note **dizzy** to a friend in a spiral inside these circle papers. (And then try to walk in a straight line!)

You will need:

Colored paper

White paper

A CD for tracing
(No CDs will be harmed during the making of these notes!)

A pencil

Scissors

Double-stick tape or glue stick

1 Trace a CD (including the hole in the middle) on a piece of colored paper, and again on a piece of white paper. Cut both out.

2 Cut the colored paper circle in half.

3 Tape or glue the half circle to the white paper circle.

4 Fold the part of the white paper that is not stuck to the colored paper over to the opposite edge.

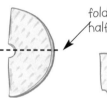

FRONT: colored paper

white paper

BACK: fold

colored paper on back

5 Fold the whole thing in half so the colored paper is on the outside.

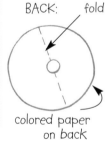

fold in half

6 Unfold and write a note inside on the white circle.

P.S. These make fun party invitations, too!

—♥ Laura

Never-Ending Note

Have all your friends write an ongoing note. It'll help you stay in touch and keep you giggling.

1 Decorate the notebook any way you like. This one I made uses supplies from office and craft stores, but you can use anything you want. I glued metal letters of each girl's initials onto a tag and threaded it through the spiral. The color of the tag is the color of the pen each girl will use.

2 Write a note to start off, and then pass the notebook among yourselves. No rules, except each girl should write in her own color so everyone can tell right away who wrote (or drew) what.

25

I know you have the  about making the team, but you

 big just for trying out! There won't be any

  when you give it your

best. You're not a  because you have

skills. Give it your  effort and watch everyone

go  ! Don't worry about  or any

other  , just be the  you are!

Hugs and  —Your name

colossal candy notes

If your friend needs something more than a little note, give her a super-size version. Use posterboard for this project, because you'll need something sturdy. Write a message on the posterboard using candy in place of some of the words. Use strong tape to hold the candy in place (don't use a toxic glue that could soak through the wrappers!). You can come up with your own messages, but here are a few ideas to get you started.

Nothing can come

you and me.

Every day is a

with you as a friend.

27

message in a bottle

You don't need an ocean to send a message in a bottle to a friend. Let the bottle "wash up" in her locker, her room, or leave it on her seat at school. This is also a great way to send an SOS when you need a friend to talk to.

You will need:

An empty, clean, non-breakable (meaning plastic) **drink bottle**

Craft sand

A note

String

Shredded paper or tinsel

Tape

Glitter, beads, or rhinestones

1 Write a note on a piece of paper and roll it up like a scroll. Tie it shut with a string.

2 Fill the bottom of the bottle with sand. Mix in a little glitter or sparkly beads or rhinestones.

3 Put the note inside the bottle. Add some shredded paper or tinsel.

4 Put it someplace where your friend is sure to find it.

If your friend likes goofy jokes, write "I'm your jean-ie in a bottle" on a piece of denim. Roll it up and stick it in the bottle.

—♥ Laura

28

matchbook surprises

Put a small gift in a little package to brighten a friend's day.

You will need:

A matchbook

Colored paper

Scissors

Double-stick tape

A sticker

A small gift (a necklace, a charm, a magnet, etc.)

1 Carefully pull out the staple that attaches the matches to the matchbook. Take out the matches and give them to an adult.

2 Cut a piece of colored paper to fit the matchbook cover. Use double-stick tape to attach the paper to the matchbook. Cut out a circle or another shape of the same paper to decorate the inside of the matchbook if you want.

3 Attach the gift to the inside of the matchbook with double-stick tape, or punch holes to tie on a necklace or charm.

4 Write a note on the inside of the top flap. Seal the matchbook shut with a sticker.

29

sneaky notes

Here's a great way to sneak a note to a friend. Don't try this method at school, though, because you might get in trouble for having gum AND passing notes.

You will need:

A pack of gum

Note cards

Scissors

Double-stick tape

2 Fold a note card in half and cut both layers the same size as the stick of gum. Wrap the note in the foil wrapper. (Go ahead and chew the gum—you won't need it for the project.)

3 Cut a long strip of note card a bit less wide than the wrapper.

4 Fanfold the strip so it fits behind the wrapper.

5 Use double-stick tape to attach the fan-folded strip to the stick of "gum."

6 Put the whole thing back in the package. Pass back and forth for an ongoing note. (Top secret, of course.)

1 Carefully unwrap one piece of gum.

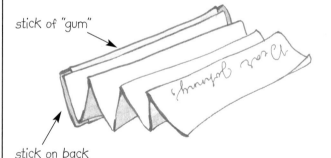

stick of "gum"

stick on back

Try writing to your friend in code to avoid peeping eyes. An easy code to do is a reverse alphabet. A = Z, B = Y, C = X, and so on.

"Meet me at lunch" would be "Nvvg nv zg ofmxs."

— ♥ *Laura*

Old-School Note Folding

Here's a tried-and-true way of folding an 8½" x 11" piece of paper into a private and compact note perfect for passing:

1
Fold the paper in half one way, and then in half the other way, so the paper is one-fourth the size of its former self.

2
Fold the paper in half the long way, and then open it back up again.

3
Fold the long edges in to the middle.

4
Fold the bottom edge up to about 1½ inches from the top edge. This will make a pocket for the top edge.

5
Fold the top edge down and tuck it inside the pocket. Pass it.

31

Pass It On! Cool Notes

charm books

Write all your secrets in these charming books you make yourself. I like to use mine to draw sketches and write down things I don't want to forget when I'm out with my friends. I also like to make my friends matching books with personalized charms.

You will need:

Colored paper

Scissors

Clear contact paper (optional)

White paper

Floss (craft floss, embroidery floss, dental floss . . . almost any kind of floss will do)

A needle

Glue

Charms (ready-made, or make them with shrink-art paper—see opposite page)

1 Cut a rectangle of colored paper to make the covers. Fold it in half to make the front and back cover.

2 If you want, stick the unfolded cover down on a piece of clear contact paper and trim all the way around it. This will make the book look good longer, especially if it gets bounced around in your purse or stuffed in your back pocket.

3 Cut five or six pieces of white paper to make the pages. You want to cut them a bit smaller than the covers. To do this, I trace the unfolded cover on the paper, then cut inside the lines by about ⅛ inch.

4 Stick the pages inside the covers and fold the whole thing in half.

5 Thread the needle with some floss. Open the book to the middle page. Hold the covers and pages together.

6 Poke the needle through the crease, right in the middle and out through the cover. Leave a floss tail a couple of inches long.

inside

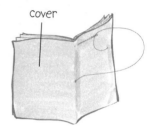

cover

7 Poke the needle up through the cover and pages at the top of the crease.

8 Poke the needle down through the pages and cover at the bottom of the crease.

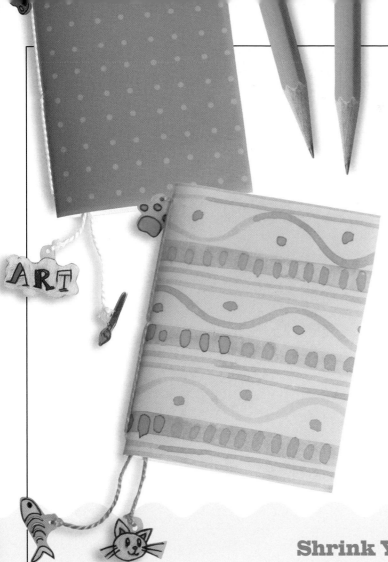

9 Thread the needle through the middle hole that's already there. Tie the floss ends in a square knot. Trim the ends. Dab a little glue on the knot so it won't come untied.

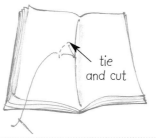

tie and cut

10 Thread a charm onto the middle of a piece of floss. Fold the floss in half and thread a needle over both ends.

11 Poke the needle through the top hole. Pull until the charm is snug against the hole on the outside of the cover.

12 Tie charms onto the ends of the floss and let them hang down the center crease. Dab a little glue on the knots so they won't come untied.

Shrink Your Art

Try making shrink-art charms. Instructions come with the plastic, which you can find anyplace that sells craft supplies.

My sister, Sherri, and I spent hours making shrink art. Shrink-art plastic used to be slick, and the only thing you could use on it was a permanent marker. We traced a lot of Snoopy and Garfield cartoons, but they were all black or blue because these were the only permanent markers our Dad had in his desk drawer.

Now, shrink-art paper is much improved because it comes with a surface on which you can use pens, pencils, and even paint. My favorite is colored pencils. My sister went nuts when this stuff came out and became a bona fide shrink-art artist.

The best part of shrink art is that even if you're not a great artist, everything looks better when it's shrunk down tiny! Plus, shrink art is fun. I think Sherri and I made all those blue Snoopys just to watch them curl up and get tiny in the oven.

backpack notes

You'll never feel far from your friend if you keep a note from her close by.

You will need:

An empty prize capsule
Thin cord
A button
A nail
A large bead
A note from your friend
Glitter or tinsel (optional)

1 Take the cap off the prize capsule. Poke a hole in the top with the nail. (You don't need a hammer—just sort of gouge it through.)

2 Thread a piece of cord through the holes in the button. Center the button on the cord.

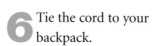

3 Thread both ends of the cord up through the hole in the cap. The button will stop the cord from slipping through the hole.

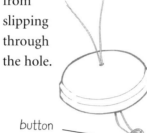

button

4 Slide a bead on both ends of the cord.

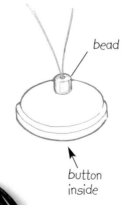

bead

button inside

5 Put the note from your friend inside the capsule. Add a little glitter or tinsel to the capsule if you want. Put on the lid.

6 Tie the cord to your backpack.

"If I could erase your problems, I would."

"No matter what, our friendship will always stick."

booster notes

If your friend needs an extra bit of attention, write her a note with a little present. Then put it in a prize capsule for her to find later. Here are some ideas.

"I'm here for you."

"You're a star."

"Sorry your day's been so hairy."

"Stick with it!"

35

Pass It On! Cool Notes

slam book

A slam *book* is something to share with as many friends as possible. Here's the idea: Take a notebook, write some interesting questions in it, and then pass it around for everyone to write in. You'll be surprised how well you'll get to know people. General slam *books* are fun, but you can also do a themed slam *book*, say, for people who love basketball or for people who are fans of certain movies, etc.

You will need:

A spiral notebook

Old magazines or catalogs that you can cut up

Scissors

Glue stick

Clear contact paper or Mod Podge

String or yarn

A pen

Duct tape (optional)

1 Cut out images, words, and letters from the magazines or catalogs that reflect the theme of your slam book. If your slam book is general, just pick images you like, or images that relate to your question. I like to cut out letters in different fonts to spell out words.

2 Glue the words and images to the front of the spiral-bound notebook collage-style. If you're going to use duct tape on the pen later (see step 4), you may want to work some into the cover design.

3 Cut a piece of clear contact paper the size of the notebook cover and stick it over your collage to protect it. Do this very carefully so you don't get any air bubbles. Start at one edge and carefully roll it down to the other end. Or paint the whole thing with a layer of Mod Podge. It won't be quite as protected, but will stick down all the loose edges.

4 Tie the string to the spiral binding, and tie a pen on the other end. You may want to wrap duct tape all the way around the pen and string to be sure it doesn't come off. Kind of outer space–looking, yet practical, too.

Fair warning: In the olden days, a slam *book* was sometimes used to write mean things about people—but of course, you would never do that. Be sure and explain that this is a friendly book!

—♥ *Laura*

Question Suggestions

- What's your favorite movie character/**TV** show/food/color/etc.?

- If you could choose any pet in the world, what would you choose?

- Would you rather be able to fly or be invisible? Why?

- If you could be a superhero, what one amazing power would you like to have?

- Is there anything you wouldn't eat for a million dollars?

- If you had to live in a cartoon, which one would you pick?

- What's the one thing you own that you would never give away?

- What's your secret talent?

37

dragonfly pencils

My BFF, Pam, and I used to sit clear across the room from each other during math class. Since we didn't know sign language, and couldn't last a whole hour without talking to each other, we'd write large notes on the back of our papers and hold them up for each other to read. Here's a better version of that method: Just clip notes to the top of these buggy pencils.

You will need:

A pencil

A mini-clothespin

Acrylic paint

A paintbrush

Glitter glue (optional)

Googly eyes

Craft glue

Scissors

Thin pipe cleaners

Thick, strong glue like E-6000

1 Paint the clothespin. It's easiest to paint one half, let it dry, and then paint the other half.

2 After the paint is completely dry, spread on a thin layer of glitter glue if you want a sparkly dragonfly. You could also spread on a thin layer of glue and sprinkle with microfine glitter.

3 Glue on googly eyes.

4 Shape wings out of a pipe cleaner. Glue the wings on the back of the clothespin.

5 Glue the dragonfly on the end of your pencil with the goopiest, heavy-dutiest glue you have. Let dry and buzz away.

Hi Heather! ☺

Mini-Clothespin Crafts

So you used a couple of mini-clothespins for the Dragonfly Pencils, and now you have almost a whole pack of them left over. Here are some fun ideas for using up the extras:

● String them on a cord, through the spring hole, with a few beads in between each clothespin. Tie knots at the end. Attach the cord to your wall, locker, or corkboard to clip stuff.

● Glue a row of clothespins on a Popsicle stick. Write names on each clothespin. Attach strong magnets to the back of the Popsicle stick for a handy-dandy locker or refrigerator magnet.

● String them up on something resembling a clothesline and hang up tiny folded paper clothes. (See page 84 for origami pajamas, dress, shirt, and purses.)

● Use them to plug your Beanie Babies' noses when something stinky is nearby.

39

YOU ROCK!

You're the Best

Go For It

Caitlin

Message Rocks

My friends and I used to go down to a river near our house and hang out. The shore was mostly rocks. We'd bring a couple of paintbrushes and some acrylic paint with us, paint a few rocks, and leave them around the shore for other people to find. We liked the idea of someone discovering one of our rocks among the others.

A fresh way to decorate a rock is to paint it totally black and let it dry, then draw or write on it with gel pens or glittery dimensional paint. I made a bunch of little ones with encouraging words ("You Rock!" and "Go For It") for a friend who had a big competition coming up. She kept some on her desk and one in her pocket for good luck.

Gifts to Make

together

Buy ingredients in bulk with a friend for a fun afternoon of creating

You will need.

Letters on paper to spell out a word *

Clear flattened marbles

Mod Podge or diluted glue

Manicure scissors (or the smallest scissors you have)

Thick, strong glue, like E-6000

A paintbrush

*(I like a black old-timey typewriter font, but you can experiment to see which fonts and colors you like.)

Bubble Word Jar

1 Paint a thin layer of Mod Podge over the letters on the paper. Press the marbles on the letters. Let dry.

2 Cut around the marbles with the manicure scissors. Turn them upside down and paint a coat of Mod Podge on the back of the letters. Let dry.

3 Lay the jar on its back and prop it in place. Glue the letters to the jar with the strongest, goopiest glue you can find. Let dry.

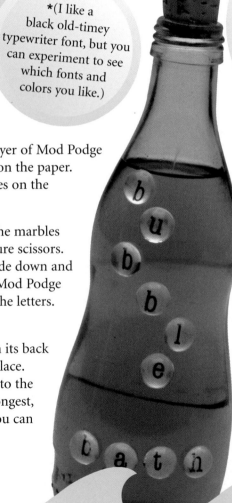

Bubble Bath

You will need.

3 cups unscented baby shampoo

1 cup glycerin (You can find it at a pharmacy.)

1/3 cup water

Essential oil or perfume (not cologne)

A funnel

1 Pour all the ingredients except the essential oil into a large container. Stir GENTLY (you don't want an out-of-control bubble fest).

2 Add the essential oil, one drop at a time, until you have a light scent. Go easy. You don't want Granny kicked out of her Gin Rummy group for reeking like a perfumerie.

3 Funnel the bubble bath into fancy jars or bottles with lids or corks.

Bath Salts

1 Pour 2 cups of Epsom salts into a container with a lid or a large plastic bag that seals.

2 Add one drop of food coloring and two drops of essential oil.

3 Put the lid on the container tightly, or seal the bag. Shake it up until

gifts for Moms, Grandmas, and other BAFs (Best Adult Friends).

Fizzy Bath Bombs

Give the gift of a scented, soft bath and fizzy fun.

You will need:
- **1 cup baking soda**
- **½ cup cornstarch**
- **1 cup citric acid** (You can find this at the drugstore.)
- **⅛ cup Epsom salts** (You can find this at the drugstore, too.)
- **½ cup olive oil**

1 Mix everything together into a big bowl except the olive oil and essential oil.

2 Add the olive oil and mush everything around until it feels like dough.

3 Add essential oil if you want (start with 10 drops and then see if it needs a little more) and mush around until it's evenly distributed.

4 Form the dough into Ping Pong–size balls. Let the bath bombs sit out overnight, then put each one in a sandwich bag tied shut with a ribbon.

You will need:
- **Epsom salts** (Look for a milk-carton–like container at the pharmacy.)
- **Liquid food coloring**
- **Essential oil or perfume** (not cologne)
- **A container with a lid or a large plastic sealable bag**
- **Jars or bottles**

Essential oil (optional)
Sandwich bags (the cheap kind without the seal)
Ribbon

the color is distributed evenly through all the salts. Add another drop if the salts need more color, and a little more essential oil if needed (remember the old saying: "Sometimes less is more"). You just want a hint of color in the salts—you don't want to turn the bathwater colors.

4 Pour into jars or bottles with lids.

Painted Glass Jars

1 To make colorful, stained-glass–like jars, make a simple outline on a jar with dimensional paint. Let it dry completely.

2 Mix 1 tablespoon of white glue with a few drops of food coloring in a paper cup.

3 Use a paintbrush to paint in the design. Wash the brush out immediately.

4 Decorate the top of the lid with a large rhinestone if you want. Let the jar dry completely before filling.

You will need:

Glass jar or a bottle with a lid

Dimensional paint

White glue

Food coloring

A paper cup

A paintbrush

You will need:

1 cup clear bubble bath or baby shampoo

2 packets unflavored gelatin
(Look for the Knox brand on the grocery shelf next to Jell-O.)

Food coloring

Small rubber ducky

Jellied Bubbles

1 Microwave 1½ cups of water (in a microwave-safe container) until it boils. Ask for parental help with this.

2 Pour the gelatin into the hot water. Stir until it is completely dissolved.

3 Stir the bubble bath or baby shampoo carefully into the gelatin and mix gently. You don't want to get the mixture all bubbly.

4 Add a drop of food coloring and mix gently again.

5 With parental help, pour into glass jars. Drop the ducky into the jar, too.

6 Put the jars in the refrigerator until the gelatin is set.

7 Tie a small spoon or scoop to the jar, along with an instruction tag that says to scoop a little out and put under warm running water for bubbles.

You can decorate the containers to make these gifts extra-personal. BAFs love to receive gifts made by you! —♥ *Laura*

Beautiful Bath Oil

You will need:

Baby oil or mineral oil
Essential oil (optional)
Food coloring
A funnel

This is a simple, beautiful gift anyone would love to receive. A beaded cork bottle makes it extra special.

1 Mix the baby oil with a drop of food coloring.

2 Add a few drops of essential oil if you want.

3 Using a funnel, pour the mixture into bottles with cork lids.

Beaded Corks

1 Cut a piece of wire about 4 inches long with the fingernail clippers.

2 Thread a bead onto the wire and curl the wire around it to hold it in place.

3 Thread on more beads, leaving at least a ½-inch tail of wire.

4 Poke the wide end of a cork onto the end of the wire.

You will need:

Cork
Fingernail clippers
Wire
Beads

sweet & fruity lip gloss

My friends and I used to be more interested in making our own custom makeup than actually wearing it. I won't tell you how to make that nasty turquoise eye shadow that Pam wore exactly once, but I will share this great recipe for lip gloss that we still make sometimes.

You will need:

Petroleum jelly

A microwave-safe container

A spoon

Pixy Stix or sweetened powdered drink mix

Clean, small containers (Find these at drug stores, or recycle small candy containers and tins, old cosmetic containers, bead containers, or other small containers with lids.)

Glue, glitter, beads, buttons, or other decorations

1 Put a blob (a large spoonful, to be inexact) of petroleum jelly in the microwave-safe container. Ask for parental permission and help. Microwave for 30 seconds. Use a hot pad and take the container out of the microwave. Stir. Put the container back in for 30 seconds. Continue doing this until the petroleum jelly is melted (it will liquefy). Be sure and take it out every 30 seconds and stir it. Be patient.

2 Add a little powder from the Pixy Stix or drink mix. Stir until the powder dissolves.

3 Spoon the mixture into the containers (which you've thoroughly cleaned and dried first).

4 Let the lip gloss get firm before you use it (a couple of hours).

5 Decorate the lid of the container. Glue on glitter or small, decorative things. You can paint candy-tin lids with acrylic paint, use stickers, or draw a design with dimensional paint.

Safety note:

This lip gloss should last a long time, but if it changes color, consistency, or smell, throw it out and whip up a new batch.

46

Best Friends Forever

beyond fruit

If you're more of a chocolaty girl than a fruity girl, you can experiment with using hot chocolate mix instead of the Pixy Stix suggested. (Not regular cocoa—too bitter!) My friend Lisa made hers this way, and she always smelled like a Hershey's Kiss. You can also try a drop of flavoring oil sold at stores that have candy-making supplies. Try adding a couple of candy red hots to the melted petroleum jelly. Stir it around so the jelly picks up the color and flavor of the candy, then throw away the unmelted parts of the candy.

Gifts to Make Together

group gifts

T-Shirt Talk

Classic and oh-so-easy, but still a perfect friendship group gift! Prewash a white T-shirt and provide permanent markers or fabric markers for guests. Have everyone write their name, a note, or a doodle. The easiest way to do this is to slide a piece of stiff cardboard inside the T-shirt to hold it taut. This also works great for items other than T-shirts, like a pillowcase, white canvas tennis shoes, or even jeans. I'm always baking cookies for my friends, and once they surprised me with an apron they'd all signed. (Very cool, but of course it was a bribe to keep making cookies.)

These gifts work perfectly when a group of friends wants to do something special for another friend (say, at a birthday party or a going-away party for a friend who is moving), or just for fun at a slumber party.

NUMBER ONE

K

GOOD LUCK!

All-My-Friends Bracelet

Make a friendship bracelet braided by all the guest of honor's friends. Start with three strands of floss or cord each about 3 feet long. Tie the strands together at one end and tape the end to a table. Have each person braid a part of the bracelet and add a bead with her initial on it. Add beads by threading a bead on one strand, and pushing it up close to the braid. Continue braiding around the bead. It doesn't matter how long the bracelet gets—it can wrap several times around the recipient's wrist. She'll always have her friends close by.

Tag Team

Buy colorful metal-rimmed tags at an office-supply store. Have each party guest write a note or draw something on a tag for the guest of honor. At the end of the party, thread all the tags on a key chain loop. It'll be excellent to keep on a backpack strap or a belt loop.

scrapbook pouch

Keep your photos and mementos safe in this pouch that's practically like a scrapbook itself. It looks so cool you'll want to make a handle so you can hang it up. This is also a great gift that a group of friends can make for someone special.

You will need:

Two plastic binder pages with pockets meant to hold business cards, trading cards, or photos

Tape

A hole punch

A plastic lanyard or other string

Two pieces of 8 ½" x 11" colored paper

Photos and mementos

1 Tape the two binder pages together with the pockets facing out and the part that attaches into the binder at the top. Punch holes all the way around the sides and bottom of the pouch.

2 "Sew" around the edges of the pouch with the plastic lanyard. Tie a knot at the end.

3 Insert the colored paper into the pouch, with the colored sides facing out. Place photos and mementos in the pockets for display.

4 Add a handle for hanging or for toting around.

Party Scrapbook

Make a scrapbook for a guest of honor at a party. Ask each person to bring something: a photo with the guest of honor, a note she wrote, a program from a play they were both in, a picture of something they both love. Set up a table with 5" x 8" notecards, colored paper, scissors, glue sticks, stickers, pens, and whatever other scrapbook materials you have. Have each guest create a page on a notecard. At the end of the party, punch a hole in the corner of each card and tie them all together with a piece of yarn.

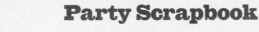

pop vase

This is a fun craft for two (especially if you just happened to have drunk sodas out of bottles with good shapes), but it's also a nice gift to make for your BFF if she's feeling down or sick. You can put a fresh flower in the vase when you're done (try a single daisy) or you can make more permanent blooms for lasting sunshine. Of course, you'll want to save the bottle caps to make the magnets on page 78.

You will need:

A soda bottle
Tissue paper
A paintbrush
Mod Podge
Scissors

1 Clean out the bottle and remove any labels. If there's sticky gunk left over, soak the bottle in warm water or use some Goof Off to get it clean.

2 Fold the tissue paper in several layers and cut out a lot of the same shapes. You can also use an extra-large–size hole punch to make shapes.

3 Paint a small section of the bottle with a thin layer of Mod Podge. Put on one tissue paper shape. Paint over the top of it with another coat of Mod Podge. Put another of the same tissue shape on top of the first one. Mod Podge over it, too.

4 Work in small sections at a time. Overlap shapes, add centers to flowers, and don't worry if you get the second tissue piece exactly on top of the first. It looks kind of cool if some are a little off.

5 Let dry. The Mod Podge will dry clear.

Spray a little perfume on the paper flowers so they smell pretty, too. —♥ Laura

dried bouquet

Dried flowers are easy. Cut flowers at the base of their stems. Make sure there is no dew or moisture on them. Tie the flowers in bundles by the stems and hang them upside down in a dark, cool place. A basement closet or a dark corner of the garage (if it's not too hot) is perfect. I've done these in my bedroom closet in a pinch. Let them hang for a week or two. When there is no more moisture left, untie them and arrange. They'll last a good long time if you keep them out of direct sunlight. They will also last longer if you spray them with hairspray. The cheap kind is best. (Proof: Nothing lasted longer than my Grandma Ruby's Aqua Net bouffant hairdo.)

Paper Flowers

Cut two or three sizes of petal shapes out of paper. The more, the better. Also cut a round center. Stick a brad through the middle of the center. Thread petals on the brad, smallest to largest, and fan them out. Wrap the end of a skinny pipe cleaner around the ends of the brad after the last petal goes on. Open the brad to hold everything in place.

53

pressed flower stickers

Use pressed flowers to make beautiful stickers for sharing with friends or decorating letters, notes, or scrapbook pages. These are even better when you've collected and pressed the flowers with your friend.

You will need:

Pressed flowers

Empty round candy tins

Clear contact paper

A pencil

Scissors

1 Clean the candy tins and remove any labels.

2 Set a tin on a piece of clear contact paper with the backing still on. Trace around the bottom of the tin. Make one circle for each sticker you want to make.

3 Cut out all the circles, just inside the lines.

4 Peel the backing off a circle. Arrange a flower on the backing.

5 Carefully return the sticky contact paper to the backing, placing it over the flower. Try not to get any air bubbles.

6 To make the tin to store the stickers, cut an extra circle out of the contact paper. Place a flower on the top of the candy tin. Remove the backing from the contact paper and press the clear circle over the top of the flower.

pressing flowers

The easiest way to press flowers is to have one of those wooden flower presses with the four screws in the corners, because you can pack it around and press flowers on the spot. You get equally good results, though, the free way. Pick flowers without any moisture or dew on them. Put the flowers between five or six layers of paper towels. Put a heavy book, like a big dictionary or phone book, on top. Now wait about two weeks and check the flowers. They are done if they feel dry and are thoroughly squashed and paper-thin.

When looking for flowers to press, pick flowers that are on the small side and not too thick. For example, a pansy will press well; a rose will not.

55

These tins filled with stickers make great gifts for moms, teachers, grandmas, and friends. —♥ Laura

framed pets

Sometimes, does it seem like your closest friends are those of the furry and feathered variety? They can't help you make these frames, but they can mug for your camera. I love this combination of silver gel pen on black acrylic paint. I use it to decorate everything from jewelry boxes to greeting cards.

You will need:

A picture frame with a flat, paintable surface (You can buy cheap plain paper frames at the craft store.)

A photograph

Black acrylic paint

A silver gel pen

1 Paint the frame with the black paint. Let dry. You may want to do another coat for better coverage.

2 Make sure the frame is completely dry. Draw on designs with the gel pen.

If you goof, the ink will wipe off if you get to it immediately. Otherwise, make it look like it belongs there.

3 Insert the photo in the frame. Meow!

Doggie Cookies

Is a dog your best friend? At my friend Jill's house, a little weenie dog named Heidi was queen. Jill's mom made Heidi rice and beef for supper every night. Heidi didn't like me (maybe because I smelled like my cat, Miko). Make your canine friend these homemade treats when you want to show how much you care, but feed him dog food the rest of the time.

6-ounce jar of beef and vegetable baby food

½ cup wheat germ

1 cup nonfat dried milk

Preheat the oven to 350 degrees. Measure all the ingredients into a bowl and stir together with a fork. Grease a cookie sheet and drop dough by small spoonfuls onto sheet. Flatten a little with the back of the fork. Bake 12–15

minutes until they are lightly browned. Let cool completely before you give them to your dog. Store them in the refrigerator in a sealed bag for up to one week. You may or may not want to warn your little brother that these are cookies for the dog.

Cat Grass

If your indoor kitty is your buddy, grow a healthy treat to bring the outside in for her. Plant some oat-grass seeds in a pot of soil, following the directions on the package. (You can find oat-grass seeds at retailers like Wal-Mart and Target, or at a pet or garden store.) Place the pot in a sunny window. When the grass is about 4 inches tall, it's ready for munching. Set the pot by the kitty's food bowl. Keep the soil moist so the grass will last.

pet collar

A pet-safe collar for Fido, a matching choker for you.
What's not to love about matching your furry friend?

You will need:

Self-stick ¾-inch-wide Velcro (enough to go around your neck and your pet's neck, plus a few inches extra)

Fabric patches or buttons

Scissors

Felt

A needle and thread

1 To make the collar (or the choker), measure around Fido's neck (or your neck) and add 2 inches. Cut the fuzzier side of the Velcro to this measurement.

2 Cut about 2 inches of the loopier, less fuzzy side of the Velcro. Stick this to the back side of one end of the fuzzy Velcro strip.

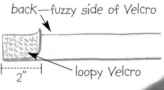

back—fuzzy side of Velcro

2"

loopy Velcro

loopy Velcro   felt

3 Cut a piece of felt to the same size as the rest of the back of the Velcro strip and stick it on.

4 Sew on a patch or button.

5 Wrap around Fido's neck and stick the Velcro together at the ends.

This is safe for your pet, because if the collar gets stuck on something, it will rip off and prevent choking.

—♥ Laura

doggie
bandanna

A pet-safe bandanna is a great way to show your BFLF (Best Four-Legged Friend) that you care. Fold down the cut edge of half a bandanna several times. If you have a small dog or cat, cut a few inches off the cut edge first. Stitch a piece of Velcro on each side, through all the layers, so you can wrap the bandanna around your pet's neck. The Velcro will come loose if the bandanna gets stuck on something, keeping Fido safe from choking.

Best Friends Forever

fun for BLFs
(best little friends)

If you find yourself baby-sitting or otherwise entertaining small fry, here are some sure-hit activities that will make you the most popular big friend on the block.

Awesome Play Clay

You will need:

1 cup flour

1/4 cup salt

2 tablespoons cream of tartar

1 cup water

2 teaspoons food coloring

1 tablespoon vegetable oil

This Play Clay is better than the stuff that comes in the cans, and it lasts a long time if you keep it in an airtight container in the fridge. Make it ahead of time, and then use it for hours of fun.

With parental supervision, mix the flour, salt, and cream of tartar in a medium saucepan. Add water, food coloring, and oil. Stir over medium heat for three to five minutes. When the mixture forms a ball in the middle of the pan, it's done. Remove the pan from the heat and let it cool. Take it out of the pan and knead it until it is smooth and doughlike.

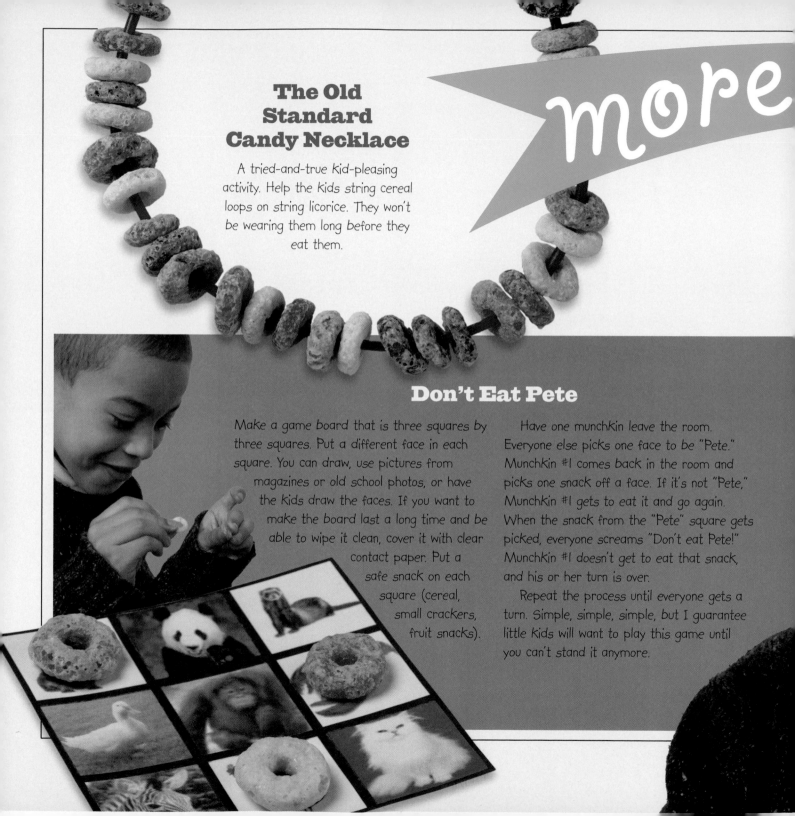

The Old Standard Candy Necklace

A tried-and-true kid-pleasing activity. Help the kids string cereal loops on string licorice. They won't be wearing them long before they eat them.

more

Don't Eat Pete

Make a game board that is three squares by three squares. Put a different face in each square. You can draw, use pictures from magazines or old school photos, or have the kids draw the faces. If you want to make the board last a long time and be able to wipe it clean, cover it with clear contact paper. Put a safe snack on each square (cereal, small crackers, fruit snacks).

Have one munchkin leave the room. Everyone else picks one face to be "Pete." Munchkin #1 comes back in the room and picks one snack off a face. If it's not "Pete," Munchkin #1 gets to eat it and go again. When the snack from the "Pete" square gets picked, everyone screams "Don't eat Pete!" Munchkin #1 doesn't get to eat that snack, and his or her turn is over.

Repeat the process until everyone gets a turn. Simple, simple, simple, but I guarantee little kids will want to play this game until you can't stand it anymore.

fun for BLFs

Finger-Lickin' Fun

Get everyone to wash their hands thoroughly. Then give each kid a pie plate or cookie sheet. Spoon a blob of pudding, or better yet, a couple of blobs in different colors, and let them fingerpaint. An activity and a snack in one!

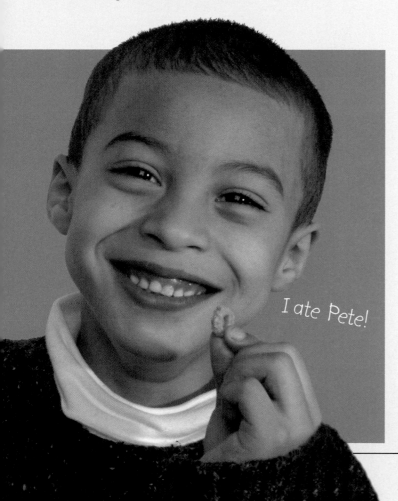

I ate Pete!

Hovercraft

Make cool Hovercrafts for your little charges and they'll think you walk on air. Ahead of time, remove a pop-top (the kind of cap you can pull up and push down) from a water bottle and glue it in the middle of an old CD. (Save the free ones that come in the mail!) Let it dry.

Let the kids decorate the CD with markers or stickers. Blow up a balloon and stretch the end over the top of the pop-top. Let a munchkin pull the pop-top lid up (with the balloon on it) and watch the hovercraft hover. It works best on a flat surface. Make a couple and have races. For safety reasons, make sure you throw away any deflated balloons so kids won't choke on them, and you do the blowing.

2-cute-4-words sock bunnies

I make a lot of things out of socks. Sock monkeys, sock snowmen, sock cats, dogs, snakes, you name it. These bunnies, however, are my friends' hands-down favorite. Make a matching set with your friend and get ready to have a cute attack.

You will need:

Two white socks

Two colored socks

Scissors

Popcorn or rice (unpopped, uncooked, of course)

Rubber bands

Black and pink felt

A needle and black thread

Glue

A button or charm (optional)

1 Fill a white sock with popcorn or rice up to the heel. Popcorn makes a squattier, fat-bottomed bunny. Rice makes a perkier, more svelte bunny. You decide. I'm partial to fat-bottoms, myself.

2 Close the top off with a rubber band. Hold the sock above the rubber band straight up. Have your friend cut it down the middle, stopping about a half-inch above the rubber band.

3 Let the strips fall to each side of the body for ears. Trim the ends in a curve so they're bunny-ear–shaped.

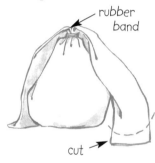

rubber band

cut

4 Cut the top off the colored sock, just above the heel.

5 Close off the cut end with a small rubber band. Cut the fabric above the rubber band into strips to make a pom-pom.

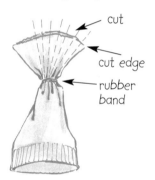

cut

cut edge

rubber band

6 Stick the hat on the bunny. Glue a button or charm to the hat if you want.

64

7 Cut a little pink nose and little round eyes out of the felt. Glue in place.

whiskers as long as you want them on the first side. Trim the thread on the other side. Put a small dab of glue at the base of the whiskers to keep them from sliding around.

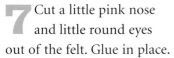

glue ← cut

8 Thread the needle with the black thread and double it. Don't tie a knot at the end. Send the needle in close to one side of the nose and out on the other side of the nose. Pull until the tails of the thread make

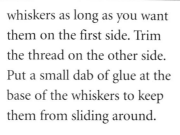

No-Sew Sock Guy

Here's my best quickie sock project. It's a perfect slumber-party activity. Have everyone bring a sock that doesn't have a mate. Cut the sock off at the heel. Fill the toe part almost full of popcorn or rice. Use a rubber band to close off the top. Glue on googly eyes and a pom-pom nose. Use a rubber band to close the cut end of the rest of the sock, and put it on for a hat.

fuzzy dudes

Everyone flips for these handmade Fuzzy Dudes, even though I'm not sure exactly what they are or what they are for. Join the fuzzy phenomenon by making a bunch for all your friends. Then watch out for people who will pretend to be your friend so they can have one, too.

You will need:

A skein of embroidery floss for each fuzzy dude

Scissors

Glue

Googly eyes

Mini-clothespins

1 Cut a piece of embroidery floss about 8 inches long. Set it aside.

2 Hold four of your fingers together (you don't need your thumb). Wrap the rest of the embroidery floss around your fingers. Don't wrap too tightly or your fingers will turn blue.

3 Carefully remove the floss from your fingers.

4 Tie the piece of floss you cut off in the beginning as tightly as you can around the middle of the looped floss.

5 Cut through all the loops on both sides.

6 Trim the thread so it's close enough to a ball.

7 Glue on googly eyes. Glue a clothespin on the back. Let dry.

pom-poms

One of the first craft projects I remember was making pom-poms out of yarn. My mom used to crochet, and she'd give me the leftover yarn. I'd make the pom-poms, and then glue them together to make animals and characters like a snowman.

If you've got some extra yarn lying around, try making these yourself. Instead of using your fingers, you can wrap the yarn around a piece of cardboard so you can get large pom-poms. If you've got a cat, leave a long string on a pom-pom and run around with it. Your cat will think it's died and gone to cat-toy heaven.

Experiment with different kinds of strings to get different effects.

67

cards for friends

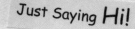

All That Glitters

Decorate a CD (instructions on page 16) and glue it to the front of a sturdy blank card. Spread glue on the rest of the card front. Sprinkle on fine glitter. Tap to remove the excess glitter.

Warm and Fuzzy Card

Glue pom-poms (instructions on page 67) onto the card. Glue on googly eyes. Cut out felt feet and glue them onto the pom-poms too, if you want.

Pajama Party Invitation

Fold some pint-size pajamas (instructions on page 84) for these fun sleepover invitations.

Clippy Card

Draw a picture of a face on the front of a blank card. Glue on embroidery-floss hair and a paper T-shirt. Clip two barrettes with your names on them (instructions on page 92) on the hair.

These cards are the answer for showing your friendship when a friend is far away or you just want to make something for her on a special occasion. They are a greeting, a gift, and a handmade show of DIY caring all rolled into one. You can't ask for anything more! When you mail these cards, you'll want to send them in a padded envelope or wrapped in bubble wrap. They'll get crushed in a regular envelope.

Bitty Bags

Make a cute double-size version of an origami purse (instructions on page 85) to glue onto a small card. Add a fancy bead or cord strap.

Fortune Teller Card

Make a spinner by following the directions on page 118, but instead of using a CD, use thin cardboard (be sure to make it small enough to fit on your card). Then attach the spinner by poking the brad through the center of the card.

Flowery Greeting

Rip a piece of tissue paper about an inch less wide than the front of a card. Glue it to the card. It doesn't have to be neat. In fact, it looks better a little rumpled. Make a paper flower (instructions on page 53) and stick the brad in the center through the card and secure. Glue the stem to the tissue. Write a greeting with glitter glue.

Flowery Greeting 2

Stick a pressed flower (instructions on page 55) onto a card with a piece of clear contact paper. Add trim around the edges of the contact paper.

69

valentine cards

Who needs boys on Valentine's Day? Show your girlfriends you care with these heart-felt cards.

Charmed

Glue a heart doily to the front of a blank card. Spread some glue around the edge of the doily and sprinkle with glitter for a sparkly border. Punch two holes through the doily and string a Leather Charm Necklace through the holes (instructions on page 138). Tie the ends inside the card and tape in place.

Heart Prints

Press your index finger on an ink pad and then onto a card, on a slight diagonal to form one half of the heart. Make another print on the opposite diagonal, with the bottoms of the prints overlapping to finish the heart.

Sweet Butterflies

Cut two hearts out of craft foam or heavy paper and decorate. Tape the hearts together, point-to-point, overlapping them a little. Use a twist-tie or a piece of pipe cleaner to make antennae to tape onto a roll of LifeSavers, then tape the LifeSavers between the two hearts.

Bottle-Cap Card

Cut two paper stripes of contrasting color to glue onto the front of a card. Glue craft foam hearts inside empty bottle caps. Glue alphabet letters onto the hearts to spell out a message. When dry, glue the bottle caps onto the stripes.

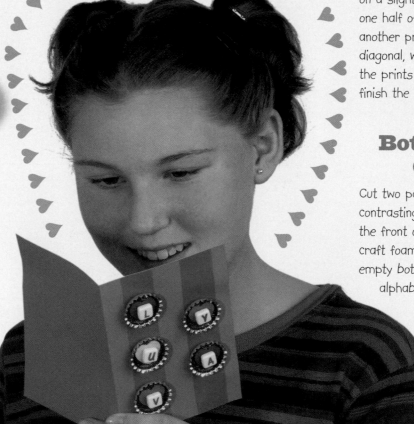

Duo Designs

for home & school

glamour girlfriends
bulletin board

If you and your friend are lucky enough to share a locker or other common space, decorate it with this diva-licious bulletin board and shiny jewel tacks.

You will need:

A plain cork bulletin board

Acrylic paint

A paintbrush

Wood letters (from the hardware or craft store)

Glitter

Glue

Faux fur trim

1 Choose letters that spell your names and paint each letter a different color. Sprinkle glitter on the letters as soon as they are painted. Let dry. Tap off the excess glitter.

2 Draw a line with a ruler down the middle of the bulletin board. Paint half the board one color and half another color. Don't worry about getting the line in the middle perfect. You won't see it. Let dry.

3 Glue the letters onto the sides of the bulletin board.

4 Glue a strip of faux fur down the middle of the bulletin board.

Don't be afraid to tap into your inner princess for this craft, but if glitter and jewels aren't your style, leave the wood letters plain and glue a piece of felt instead of fur down the middle.

— ❤ *Laura*

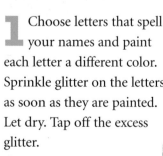

flashy tacks

For tacks worthy of the board, glue jumbo flat-backed rhinestones to large thumbtacks. Use the thickest, goopiest glue you can find. Let dry thoroughly.

CHAPTER 3
FRIENDS

hip to be square tacks

The hardware store is a treasure trove for crafts. You can pick up a sheet of these mini-tiles for a couple of bucks, and have more than enough to share with all your friends.

You will need:

White matte (that means NOT glossy) **mini-tiles**

Scissors

Dimensional squeeze paints

Mod Podge or white glue

Acrylic paint

A paintbrush

Tiny doodads, tiny pictures cut from magazines, or photocopies

Thick, strong glue like E-6000 or Plumber's Goop

Large, flat-backed thumbtacks

1 Cut the tile pieces apart. Scrape off any remaining gummy stuff with the edge of your scissors.

2 Get creative. Here are a few tips: To make a colored background, paint the tile with two coats of acrylic paint (yes, you have to let it dry between coats). Glue on tiny objects and decorate with dimensional paint, or decoupage on a paper picture. To do this, paint a coat of Mod Podge or diluted glue (see page 21) onto the tile. Stick on the picture. Paint another coat of Mod Podge or glue over the top.

3 When your tile art is finished and dry, turn the tiles over and glue on tacks with the goopiest, strongest glue you have. Let the glue dry (probably overnight—read the label) and go tack something up.

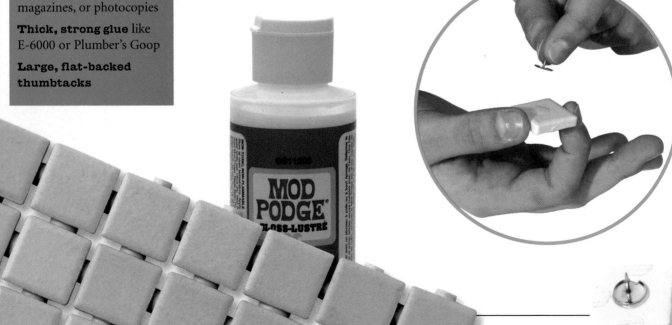

Coaster Corkboards

Show off your square tacks with these round, stick-anywhere corkboards. Get cork coasters at craft and hardware stores.

1 Bend the very end of a pipe cleaner into an "L" shape.

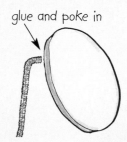

glue and poke in

2 Dab a little glue on the end of the pipe cleaner and poke it into the side of a coaster.

3 Wrap the pipe cleaner tightly around the coaster.

4 Bend the other end in an "L" shape and put a little glue on it. Stick it in the cork right next to the other end. Hold the ends for a few minutes until the glue sets.

5 Hang with heavy-duty mounting tape.

75

footnotes

Either you or a friend will have to sacrifice a pair of toe socks, or you can go in together and buy a pair. You'll each have a toe-riffic pencil holder.

You will need:

A pair of toe socks

Rice (uncooked, but you knew that, right?)

A lid, cup, or jar, approximately 2 inches wide and 2 inches deep (A wide hairspray-can lid works great.)

1 Fill each sock about ¾ full with rice. Make sure you shake the rice down into all the toes.

2 Put the lid, cup, or jar inside the opening of the sock for the pencil holder part.

76

Best Friends Forever

If your mom, aunt, or friend's mom had her best years in the 1980s, you might find some things deep in their closets that are crafting treasures waiting to surface. For instance, toe socks were popular in the '80s, along with clunky early-Madonna jewelry and Jordache jeans (it's best not to ask Mom if she still fits in them).
I found Smurfs on key chains and re-did them to look like my friends. They were very funny, if you don't mind being blue. If you find an Alf doll, a Def Leppard CD, or stonewashed parachute pants, leave them exactly where you found them and back away carefully. Some things are best left alone.

Play with Your Pencils

1 Tightly coil a pipe cleaner around the top fourth of a pencil. Don't overlap the coils. Hold on to the bottom of the coil and pull the top end just enough to make a springy end on the pencil. Boing!

2 Wrap the end of a pipe cleaner tightly around the top of a pencil. Starting at the other end, twirl it into a spiral.

3 Try zig-zags and different shapes. Let your imagination go fuzzy!

77

Duo Designs for Home & School

bottle-cap locker magnets

Think of these locker magnets as mini displays for small 3-D items or pictures of friends. Once you make some, you might be tempted to drink way too many root beers just to get the caps. Better idea: Next time you have a party, serve soda in bottles with caps. Snitch the caps before you pass out the sodas.

You will need:

Bottle caps

Double-sided tape or craft glue

Pictures of your friends and other little things to go in the bottle caps

Colored paper

A pencil

Scissors

Heavy-duty round magnets (They're cheap at the hardware store.)

1 Trace around a bottle cap on the colored paper. Cut it out just inside the line.

2 Attach the paper to the inside of the bottle cap with double-stick tape or a thin layer of craft glue.

3 Glue in an object. If the thing you want to use is flat, glue a pony bead or small piece of craft foam or mounting tape underneath it so it pops out a little. For pictures, you can glue them to the background paper, then squirt a circle of glue around the edges for a frame. Sprinkle some glitter or small beads into the glue. Tap out the excess.

4 No need to glue the magnet to the back of the bottle cap. Just stick the magnet on your locker, then stick on the bottle cap. If you've got more bottle caps than magnets, create a rotating display.

DIY Sacrifices

Sometimes a girl has to do what a girl has to do—especially when she must have something for crafting. I once found some sodas from Mexico with the all-time best bottle caps. I bought a six-pack. The label said the soda had a kick, but I wasn't quite prepared for the berry-flavored soda with a tomato-y, Tabasco-sauce–hot aftertaste. I made my friends try it, too, as an excuse to pop the tops. They're still my friends, but just barely.

I can't stand to waste anything, so when I buy something that I just want a part of, I try to use the rest of whatever it is. I once bought a watch that I wasn't crazy about because the tin that it came in was to die for, and little containers of beads that I didn't need because I had plans for the containers. I use lots of alphabet pasta in crafts, and when most of the good letters are gone, I cook the rest. My soup is full of leftover consonants like Xs and Ks. My cats have a lot of interesting toys made from stuffed parts of leftover clothing from other projects. And my friends know I might bring a bowl of unwrapped candies to a party because I wanted the wrappers for a project. They steer clear of any suspicious drinks, though.

pocket notebook

If you have to carry around a notebook all year for school, you might as well make it something special. You'll need to score an old pair of pants with great pockets to get started. I lucked out at the thrift store and found a pair of Boy Scout shorts for two bucks. Great shape, great material, and very cool Boy Scout buttons.

cool Boy Scout button

You will need:

An old pair of shorts or pants with pockets

Scissors

Glue

Colored paper

Double-stick tape

Notebook

Optional: craft foam, fabric patches, fabric paint, etc.

1 Cut a piece of colored paper to fit the front of your notebook. Place double-stick tape all around the edges of the notebook and stick on the paper.

2 Cut a pocket from the pants.

3 Glue the pocket to the front of the notebook.

4 Decorate the pocket any way you want. I wanted to set off the button on this pocket, so I cut a craft-foam flower and cut a small hole in the center so it would stretch over the button and stay snug.

Flipbook

If you have a notebook that you'll be taking notes in all year (and you won't be ripping out pages), do what Pam did in her notebooks: Make little flipbooks to entertain your friends. On each page, in the lower right-hand corner, draw a stick figure doing some sort of action. Each picture should show just a slight change in movement. Keep it simple. Stick figures work well with just a few details. Make sure you have action, but again, keep it simple. Each page should have just a slight change.

    Here's an example.

good luck boxes

Store fortunes, lucky pennies, or good-luck wishes from each other in these lavish little boxes.

You will need:

An empty matchbox

Origami or other colorful paper

Double-stick tape

A small hole punch

Embroidery floss

Two beads with large holes (Pony beads work well.)

Scissors

Glue

1 Cut a piece of paper to fit all the way around the outside of the box. Cut it so it fits the box exactly. No sloppiness allowed here.

2 Stick a piece of double-stick tape down the middle of the bottom of the box.

3 Carefully line up the paper with the edges of the box. Stick one edge of the paper on half the tape, wrap, then stick down the other edge of the paper onto the other half of the tape.

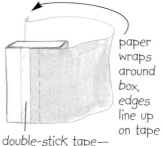

paper wraps around box, edges line up on tape

double-stick tape— half underneath paper

4 Cut pieces of paper to fit on the visible ends of the inside box. Stick the paper on with the tape.

5 Cut a different piece of paper to fit inside the box (or the same piece of paper if you want it to match). Do this by tracing the outline of the bottom of the box on the paper, then cut just inside the lines. Double-stick tape it in place.

6 Punch a hole in the front of the box. Cut embroidery floss into ten 6-inch lengths. Thread the

floss through the hole in one bead. Fold the floss in half, so all the ends are together and the bead is in the middle of the strands. Thread all the ends through the hole in the box, from the inside out.

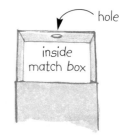

hole

inside match box

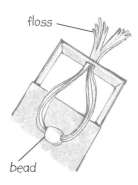

floss

bead

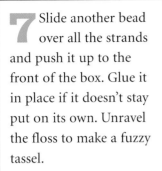**7** Slide another bead over all the strands and push it up to the front of the box. Glue it in place if it doesn't stay put on its own. Unravel the floss to make a fuzzy tassel.

8 If you already know how to make a cool origami shape, go ahead and make a mini one. One-fourth of a piece of origami paper is about the right size, or about 2" x 2". If you are not already a paper-folding genius, check the next page for a few projects.

9 Glue your masterpiece to the top of the box. May your friendship be full of good fortune!

easy origami projects

Pinwheel

1 Fold two edges to the middle of the paper.

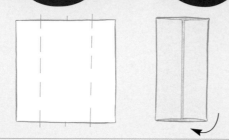

2 Fold the two short edges in to the middle.

3 Pull the corners out into little triangles.

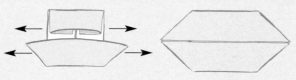

4 Bend the top right triangle up as shown.

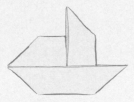

5 Bend the bottom left triangle down to finish.

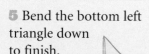

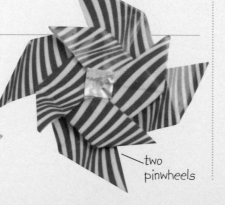

two pinwheels

Pajama Top

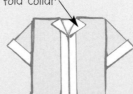

wrong side (white)

1 Start with a piece of square origami paper. Fold in half and unfold.

2 Fold just the edges of two sides out as shown. Fold sides in to middle.

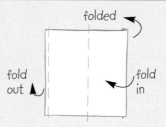

folded

fold out ▲   fold in

right side

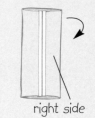

3 Fold in half, top to bottom, so the seams are on the outside front and back.

4 Fold the corners at the bottom of the seam out.

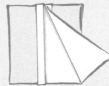

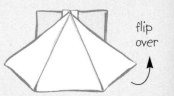

flip over

5 Flip over. Fold the corners at the top out to form a collar.

fold collar

6 Bend the top corners at the shoulders back to round them off.

Use these folded designs to top a Good Luck Box, or fold some jammies for slumber party invitations. I once made a mini-closet out of an empty candy tin and filled it with origami clothes. Have fun!

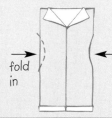

Pajama Shorts

1 Start with a square piece of origami paper. Fold the top and bottom edges out as shown.

2 Flip over. Fold the paper in half. Unfold.

fold edges into center

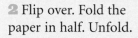

3 Fold the side edges in to the middle.

fold in

4 Fold in the middle again, so the edges are on the inside.

5 Fold diagonally in half to make shorts.

Dress

1 Start with a square piece of paper. Fold just the bottom edge out.

2 Flip over. Fold in half. Unfold.

3 Flip over. Fold side edges in to middle.

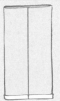

4 Bend the corners at the top down to form a collar.

5 Fold the side edges in slightly to form a waist.

fold in

6 Glue on some bead buttons. Cut small slits to make armholes if you want to hang the dress on a tiny wire hanger. To make a hanger, bend a piece of wire as shown above.

Purse

1 Cut a piece of origami paper to 1½ inches x 2½ inches.

2 Fold the bottom edge up one inch.

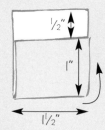

½"

1"

1½"

3 Fold the corners of the top edge down.

4 Fold the top down. Glue a bead on the front flap.

Duo Designs for Home & School

fun stickers

Stickers are the easiest way to decorate everything from your locker to your notebooks to your lampshade. What's even better is this recipe to make your own original stickers. I made these from photocopies of vintage fruit crate labels, but my favorites are the ones made from my friends' own artwork.

You will need:

- **2 tablespoons white glue**
- **1 tablespoon white vinegar**
- **A paper cup**
- **A plastic spoon**
- **A paintbrush**
- **Paper with images on it**

1 Mix the glue and the vinegar in the paper cup with the spoon until well blended.

2 Paint the solution on the back of the paper. Let it dry.

3 Now your whole paper is a sticker! Cut out the pictures (easiest in squares).

4 Moisten the backs to stick 'em. I wouldn't lick them. Glue and vinegar—yucky and probably not good for you. Use a wet cloth or a sponge or whatever is handy that you can moisten.

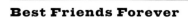

bandanna pencil cases

One bandanna equals two of these bright pencil cases.

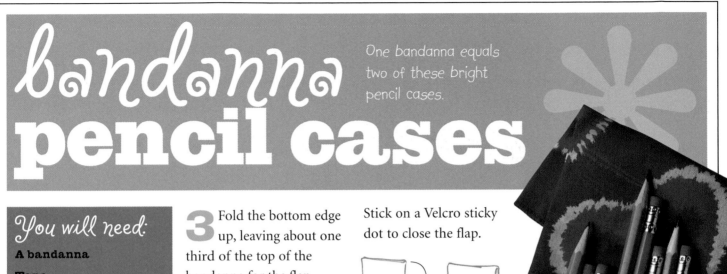

1 Stick a piece of tape on the bandanna so that one edge of the tape divides the bandanna exactly in half. Cut the bandanna in half, using the edge of the tape as a guide. Remove the tape.

2 Fold one piece of the bandanna in half the long way. Glue the edges together with the fabric glue. Let dry.

3 Fold the bottom edge up, leaving about one third of the top of the bandanna for the flap.

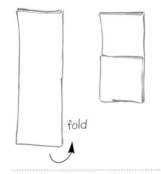

fold

4 Glue the edges together with the fabric glue. Place a phone book or other heavy book on top of the pencil case until the glue is dry.

5 Fold the top edge down about an inch above the pocket.

Stick on a Velcro sticky dot to close the flap.

fold here

6 Glue on a button or flat-backed rhinestone.

87

Duo Designs for Home & School

pocket pillows

All you need for these two pillows is one old pair of jeans. The scruffier, the better.

You will need:

One pair of old jeans

Scissors

A needle and thread

Fabric glue

Stuffing

Acrylic paint or fabric paint

Stencils and a paintbrush

Microfine glitter (optional)

Rick-rack or other trim

1 Cut the back pocket from the jeans. Cut all the way through the pants so the fabric is still behind the pocket.

2 Stencil designs on the pocket. Sprinkle on glitter while the paint is still wet if you want a little sparkle. Set the pockets aside to dry.

3 Cut about a foot off the bottom of each jeans leg.

4 Turn one pant leg inside out. Sew a seam along cut edges about ½ inch from the edges. Turn right side out.

5 Stuff the pillow.

6 Sew a seam along the open end to close the pillow.

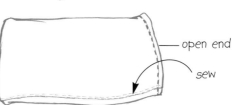

open end

sew

7 Glue the pocket to the front of the pillow with fabric glue. Let dry.

8 Glue rick-rack or other trim over the seam and top of the pocket with fabric glue.

88

Friendship

fashions

hair sticks

I have friends who pay a lot of money for these hair accessories, and they aren't nearly as cute as the ones you can make yourself. Next time you have Chinese food, ask for an extra set of chopsticks, and you and a friend can each make one for free.

You will need:

Chopsticks

Craft floss (Embroidery floss works fine, but craft floss works a little better because it has only one strand. It makes for cleaner gluing and wrapping.)

Glue

Scissors

Beads, fabric paint, or whatever you want to use to decorate the stick

1 Put a dab of glue at the top of the chopstick.

2 Stick the end of the floss in the glue. Smooth it down with your finger. (You'll get your finger gluey. If it bothers you, go wash it off before you continue.)

3 Wrap the floss tightly around the chopstick. Make sure you don't leave any gaps between wraps.

4 When you have wrapped about ⅓ of the stick, hold the floss securely in place and clip off the end.

5 Glue the end of the floss to the chopstick. Let dry.

6 Decorate your hair stick.

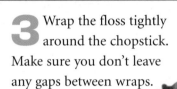

Tips!

● **Dip the end of the stick in glue, then dip it again in microbeads or glitter.**

● **Paint pasta alphabet letters, then stick them on with glitter glue.**

● **Hold two pieces of floss together to make a colorful wrap.**

● **Tie on a few beads.**

stick
style

Gather your hair in a ponytail on the back of your head. Secure it with an elastic. Twist the ponytail a few times and wrap it around the elastic so it makes a bun. If you have short hair, stop here and use a few *bobby pins* to keep everything in place. If you have long hair, push two fingers through the center of the bun and grab the rest of the ponytail. Pull it through the middle of the bun, like a knot. Leave the ends of the ponytail free.

Push a hair stick in one side of the bun, through the elastic, and out the other side. Add as many as you want and can fit.

Friendship Fashions

picture clippies

Show true friendship by wearing your BFF's photo in your hair. Buy the things you need together and your loyal style will be twice as nice.

You will need:

Snap-style hair barrettes

Tiny paper photos, graphics, or words

Clear flattened marbles

Mod Podge or diluted glue (see page 21)

A paintbrush

Manicure scissors (or the smallest pair you can find)

Thick, strong glue like E-6000

1 Paint a coat of Mod Podge on top of a picture.

2 Press a marble onto the picture, making sure there are no air bubbles. Let dry.

3 Trim the paper off around the marbles with the manicure scissors.

4 Glue each picture marble onto the end of a clippy. Let dry.

With tiny scissors, trim closely around glued-on marbles.

I call this one my hippy clippy.

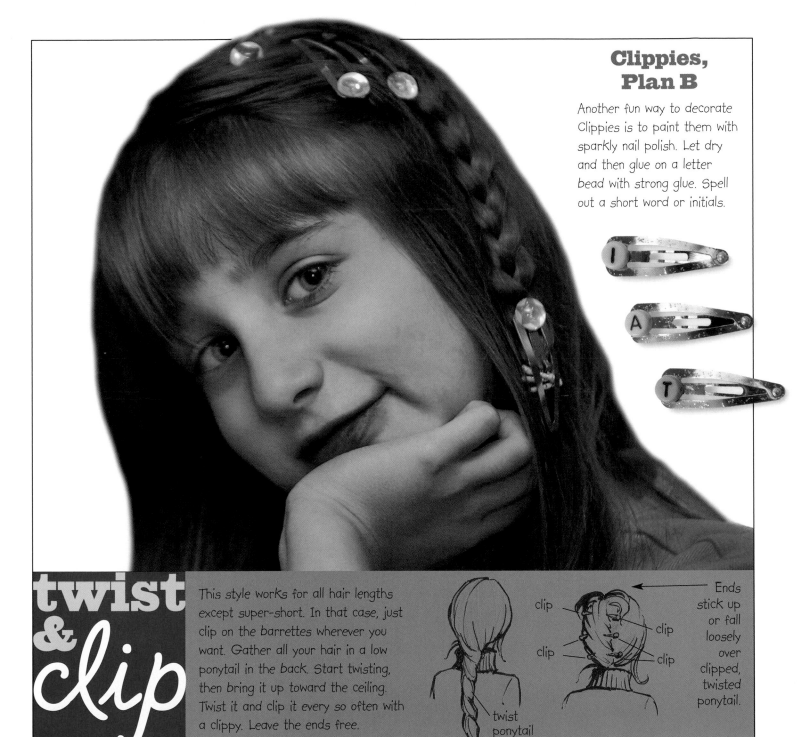

Clippies, Plan B

Another fun way to decorate Clippies is to paint them with sparkly nail polish. Let dry and then glue on a letter bead with strong glue. Spell out a short word or initials.

twist & clip

This style works for all hair lengths except super-short. In that case, just clip on the barrettes wherever you want. Gather all your hair in a low ponytail in the back. Start twisting, then bring it up toward the ceiling. Twist it and clip it every so often with a clippy. Leave the ends free.

clip

clip

twist ponytail

clip

clip

clip

Ends stick up or fall loosely over clipped, twisted ponytail.

Friendship Fashions

beaded bandannas

Bandannas are one of my favorite craft materials because they're colorful, cheap, and easy to get. I'll bet if you dig around in your dresser drawer, you'll find one you can share with your friend.

You will need:

A bandanna

Tape

Scissors

Fabric or craft glue

Pins

A needle

Two colors of embroidery floss

Small pony beads

1 Stick a piece of tape from one corner of the bandanna to the diagonal corner, so the top edge of the tape divides the bandanna in two equal pieces.

2 Cut the bandanna in half, using the tape as a guide. Remove the tape.

3 Fold the cut edge under about ¼ inch. Pin in place.

4 Fold the edge of the fabric under another ¼ inch. Pin in place.

beads

embroidery floss stitches

5 Thread the needle with a long piece of embroidery floss. Tie a knot at the end. Sew a line of stitches close to the folded edge of the fabric, through all the fabric layers. Add a bead on each stitch.

bead

first color floss (yellow)

second color floss (pink)

CRAFT THREAD DMC

Best Friends Forever

6 Tie a knot at the end and trim off the tail of embroidery floss.

7 Thread the needle with the other color of embroidery floss. Tie a knot at the end. Poke the needle up through the fabric at one end of the row of stitches.

8 Weave the needle under and around each stitch without going through the fabric.

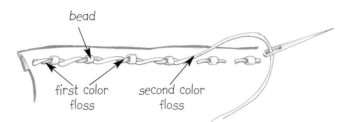

bead

first color floss

second color floss

9 Poke the needle down through the fabric at the end and tie a knot. Trim the floss.

Belt-Loop Barrettes

After you've used up all the parts of your old jeans you thought possible on Do-It-Yourself projects, there's still one more thing you can use: the belt loops. Cut off the belt loops and glue them to plain barrettes. Leave them as is, or write your names on them or draw designs with fabric or acrylic paint. Let dry and wear 'em with pride. You are true DIY girls.

pajama pant swap

This project works best if one of you can sew with a sewing machine, or if one of you has a parental person who is willing to sew for you. Straight seams, nothing complicated. If there is no sewing machine, a needle and thread and your own two hands work just fine. This project is so fabulous, it's worth the extra time.

You will need:

A friend with a pair of pajama pants that are as wide in the legs as your own pair of pajama pants

A sewing machine and someone who knows how to operate it, or a needle and thread

Tape

Sharp scissors

Pins

1 Stack the pajama pants and smooth them out. Check to make sure the bottoms of the legs are the same width.

stacked pants

2 Pin the pajama legs together and smooth out again. Stick a piece of tape across the legs where you want to cut.

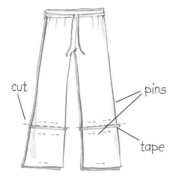

cut

pins

tape

3 Do not attempt this step unless you have sharp scissors. Dull scissors will frustrate you and mess up this project. Cut along the top edge of the tape. This will help you cut a straight line. No second chances.

4 Unpin the pajama legs and take off the tape.

5 Turn the cut-off ends of the pajama pants inside out. Pin them to the opposite pair of pants, matching the side seams. Pin in place.

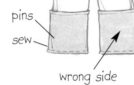

pins

sew

wrong side

6 Sew around the pant legs, about ½ inch from the edges.

7 Remove the pins, fold down the legs, iron if necessary (get a parental person to help you with this), and you've got two-of-a-kind pajama pants.

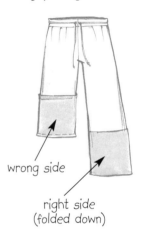

wrong side

right side (folded down)

Bunny Slippers

You will need one white regular-size washcloth and two pairs of flip-flops to make these funny Bunny Slippers. Cut the washcloth into fourths. With each fourth, make a bunny:

1 Fold in half so the cloth makes a triangle.

2 Roll up the cloth, starting at the corner.

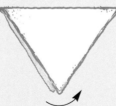

3 Bend the roll in the middle and cross the ends over each other.

4 Tie the ears in place with a ribbon. Glue on googly eyes and a pom-pom nose. Use strong, goopy glue to glue the bunnies onto flip-flops. Let dry.

twin tees

Transform dull, regular Tees into reverse matching two-of-a-kind designer duds. To start, find two T-shirts that you and your friend own that are the same width across. Then find a parental person with a sewing machine if neither of you has one. You can sew these by hand, too.

You will need:

Two T-shirts that are the same width

Tape

Scissors

A sewing machine or a needle and thread

Pins

1 Lay the T-shirts on top of each other, and decide where you want to make the cut. Smooth out the shirts and pin them together above and below where the cut will be made.

2 Stick a long piece of tape across the top of the T-shirt where you want to cut.

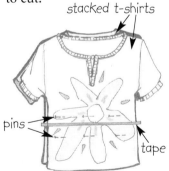

stacked t-shirts

pins

tape

3 Cut the T-shirts, using the tape as a guide. Remove the tape.

4 Turn one bottom piece inside out. Take the opposite top piece and put it inside the bottom piece, so the cut edges are even. Pin in place.

wrong side

wrong side

5 Use the sewing machine, or hand sew, about ½ inch from the edges. Tie off with a good knot and trim the thread.

6 Turn the bottom right side out and you've got a new T-shirt.

Other Ways to Match T-Shirts:

Blow It:

● **Fabric blow-pens.** These are fun, fun, fun—and you don't have to be neat. You can sign your names on the back, make big, colorful swirls, or go polka-dotty.

Bleach It:

● **Take colored shirts outside and spread them on a plastic garbage bag. Stick another garbage bag inside each T-shirt so your design won't run through the layers. Arrange leaves, sticks, flowers, and other flat things on the shirt. Ask a parental person to spray bleach all over the shirt. Let it sit until you see the bleach start to lighten the fabric. Use latex gloves to remove the nature stuff and rinse the bleach out of your T-shirt. (Rinse well—otherwise your shirt will disintegrate.)**

Print It:

● **If you or your friend has access to an ink-jet printer, you can buy T-shirt transfer paper at the computer-supply store, and iron on any design you can print off the computer.**

Write It:

● **Another cool bleach trick:** For a couple of bucks, you can find a bleach "pen" in the laundry section of a store that carries cleaning supplies (I had luck at both **Wal-Mart** and **Big K**). Use the pen (under parental supervision, of course) to draw designs on a dark shirt. Put a plastic bag inside the shirt where you are drawing so it doesn't soak through to the other side. When the fabric lightens, rinse well.

99

Friendship Fashions

knit tote bags

Got one old sweater with two sleeves or two sides? You and your friend can make matching knit bags. Très chic!

You will need:

An old sweater

Cord

Tape

A needle and thread

Scissors

Beads or buttons

1 Cut the ends off each sleeve of the sweater. Six inches from the end is about right. Turn the pieces inside out.

2 Sew across the cut end, about half an inch from the edges. Tie a knot, and then stitch another seam on top of the first one for extra strength.

wrong side

Sew 2 rows of stitches.

sew → ← sew

tape ← → tape

3 Put tape on the ends of the cord if they fray. Sew the ends halfway down the sides of the bag to make a handle.

4 Turn the bags right side out. Sew on buttons or beads for decoration. Make each bag look the same or different, depending on how matched you and your friend want to be.

larger bag ——

drawstring bag

Variations

For a larger bag, use an old cardigan and cut as shown.

Follow the regular directions, but you'll have to sew up the side seam as well.

To make a drawstring bag instead of one with a handle, turn the top edge of the bag down over a piece of cord and sew the edge to the purse, leaving a small opening for the drawstring and making sure not to sew through the cord.

cut

top of bag

wrong side folded over, cord inside

right side

pocket purses

When I go to the thrift store or garage sales with friends, we keep an eye out for clothing with great-looking pockets to make matching bags. Think outside of the denim box. Jean pocket purses are boring. Bermuda shorts with big side pockets are a better find than Levi's.

You will need:

A piece of clothing with pockets

Scissors

Cord

Tape

A needle and thread

1 Cut pockets out of the clothing. Cut completely through the fabric so the pockets still have the fabric on the back.

2 If the cord you have frays easily, wrap the ends with clear tape.

3 Put the ends of the cord down into the pocket a couple of inches. Sew in place.

4 Done!

People always notice these funky purses and wonder where I got them. It'll be our secret that they're cut from old clothes and take about five minutes to make!

— ❤ *Laura*

pant leg bags

If you found pants with good pockets, but the pockets are too small to be bags on their own, make these easy versions:

1 Cut about 12 inches off the end of the pant leg.

2 Turn it inside out and sew the cut edges together. Turn right side out.

3 Glue the pocket onto the front of the bag with fabric glue, or sew it on if the fabric's not too thick.

4 Sew the ends of the cord inside the sides of the bag for a handle.

103

Friendship Fashions

beach tote

Matching Beach Totes are cool to use when you head out to catch some rays. If you go in on the materials with your friend, they're economical, too. Great fashion should always be so cheap and easy.

You will need:

Two dish towels (I got these in a set of two at the dollar store.)

A needle and thread

Pins

Scissors

Clear tubing from the hardware store, 4 feet for each bag

Colored craft sand or actual beach sand (Just make sure it's completely dry.)

Duct tape

Funnel

1 Fold down each short end of the dishtowel an inch and a half. Pin in place.

2 Sew the edges in place to create a sleeve for the handles.

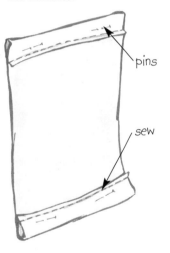

pins

sew

3 Cut the tubing into two 2-foot sections.

4 Thread one piece of tubing through one sleeve. Duct tape off one end.

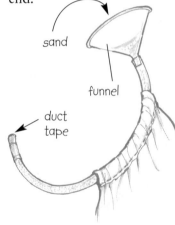

sand

funnel

duct tape

5 Use the funnel to pour sand into the tube, leaving 2 to 3 inches unfilled.

6 Remove duct tape. Cut a ½-inch slit on one end of the tubing. Push this end into the uncut end. Push it in as far as you can, twisting a little.

7 Wrap duct tape securely around the joint. Twist the handle around so the duct-taped part is hidden inside the sleeve.

8 Make the other handle the same way.

Instead of making a traditional sand castle next time you're at the beach with your friends, make mini-versions of yourselves. Use wet sand to mold a body shape (as if you were lying down on the sand). Use pebbles for eyes, find seaweed or sticks for hair, and make a seashell swimsuit. Or give yourselves tails instead of legs and make yourselves into mermaids.

My friends and I like to make sand turtles. They're quick (especially if you have a bowl or bucket for a mold for the shell) and fun to decorate with pretty rocks and shells.

9 Fold the bag in half, wrong sides out. Pin the sides of the bag together.

10 Sew a seam up each side to the handle sleeve, about ½ inch from the edges.

11 Turn the bag right side out and throw in your sunscreen and a good book.

stop here

stop here

sew

wrong side

sew

105

Friendship Fashions

zipper pulls

You and a friend can zip up a match with these easy jacket Zipper Pulls.

You will need:

A clip

Plastic lace

Two colors of pony beads

Alphabet beads

Scissors

1 Cut a piece of lace about 2½ feet long. Fold it in half and thread both ends through the clip and then through the lace loop. Pull tight.

clip

lace

2 Thread the ends of the lace through one bead in opposite directions. Pull until snug.

3 Thread the ends of the lace through two beads in opposite directions. Continue in the following pattern:

4 Tie both ends in a single knot at the end. Thread a few beads on each end of the lace and tie knots to hold them in place. Trim lace.

5 Clip on and zip!

Plastic Lace Trick

If you've beaded too tight (almost everyone does this at the beginning) and the zipper pull is bunched up instead of flat, soak the whole thing in warm water for about ten minutes. Take it out and put something heavy on top while it dries. It'll stay flat when it's dry.

boarding gloves

My friend Pam and I used to exchange one of our earrings, socks, or gloves so we'd have an unmatched, matched set. Take this one step further by personalizing your gloves before you switch them.

You will need:

One pair of gloves each

Fabric paint in a squeeze tube

Beads

A needle and thread

1 Decorate your pair of gloves with fabric-paint initials. Let dry.

2 Sew on a bead or two. Now swap one with your friend.

pairs to share:

- **Socks:** Buy almost-matching socks and swap one.

- **Shoelaces:** Pull out your shoelaces, write a *loooong* note on one, and give it to a friend. She can do the same for you.

- **Flip-Flops:** If you and your BFF wear the same shoe size, buy two pairs of cheap flip-flops. Decorate them by using a strong glue to attach fake flowers, foam cut-outs, fabric butterflies, or glitter. Use your imagination, but make sure nothing pokes your toes when you put them on. Then swap one for a perfectly mismatched set.

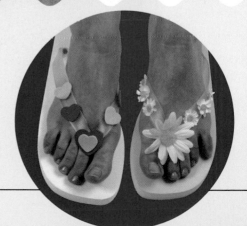

penny pouch

Wear this pouch on your jeans with a lucky penny from your best friend inside. Don't leave home without it!

You will need:

A pair of old socks
(They can have holes in the toes or heels—you only need the tops.)

Scissors

A needle and thread

Embroidery floss

Found pennies (You have to find them on the ground, or they're not lucky. Finding them in your change purse doesn't count.)

Charm or bead
(optional)

Dimensional paint
(optional)

1 Cut the top 3 inches off the socks.

2 Turn one top inside out. Sew a seam across the bottom.

3 Turn the pouch right side out.

4 Thread the needle with an 18-inch piece of embroidery floss. Double the floss and tie a knot at the end.

5 Sew a line of long stitches about ½ inch from the top of the pouch. Leave a long tail of floss at the beginning.

6 On the last stitch, thread on a bead or charm if you want.

7 Cut the needle off the floss. Tie a knot in the end of the floss.

8 Decorate the penny you find with dimensional paint if you want, and let it dry. Trade pennies with your friend.

you lucky girl

Pennies are the easiest lucky thing to find, especially in grocery store parking lots and on the floor at the mall.

I like to find four-leaf clovers and press them (*see Pressing Flowers on page 55*). I put the pressed clover on a paper background and put clear contact paper over the top. I use them for bookmarks or to give to someone who needs some luck. I also really, really love Lucky Charms cereal. I don't know if it brings good luck, but it's a happy way to start the day!

Pam kept a rabbit's foot on a key chain, which she said really, truly brought her luck when she rubbed it. I didn't want to touch it because it gave me the creeps. I once saw a reprint of an old billboard for Burma-shave that said: "On curves ahead, remember sonny, that rabbit's foot didn't save the bunny."

Speaking of unlucky animals, when I was a kid and we had chicken or turkey for dinner, my sister and I used to save the wishbone and dry it out. Then we would each grab a side and pull. Whoever got the top of the wishbone on the end of their bone got good luck. I never got it, and thought I was reduced to a life of the unlucky. My sister told me recently that she used to cheat by holding the bone with her thumb closer to the top than mine, ensuring it would break in her favor. Hmm. Guess I won't be sharing my Lucky Charms with her anytime soon.

My mom bakes a walnut in the Thanksgiving pumpkin pie every year. Whoever gets the walnut wins a prize, plus good luck all year.

— ♥ *Laura*

109

flip-flop
key chain

Share a pair of custom-designed-by-you shoes. I got addicted to designing these shoes and now they outnumber real shoes in my closet!

1 Trace the flip-flop pattern here and cut it out.

2 Trace each of the patterns on two colors of craft foam. Cut out.

3 Stack the foam pieces and glue together. Choose a strap variation from the next two pages.

4 After you've finished the shoes, punch a hole in the heel and thread a key chain through.

You will need:

Two or more colors of **craft foam** (The shimmery, self-adhesive kind works great.)

Scissors

Glue

A pencil

Wire (24- or 26-gauge), **beads, embroidery floss, glitter,** etc.

A small hole punch

Key chain

trace this pattern onto your craft foam

beaded straps   criss-cross straps   floss straps

You can make a super-chunky pair of flip-flops with a lot of layers of foam. Follow the regular directions, but punch holes in each layer before you glue them together. Also, cut out each piece of foam individually, not in a stack. (Tempting, I know, but you won't get good results. I know this from sad experience.)

STRAP VARIATIONS

Beaded Straps

1 For each shoe, fold a 6-inch piece of wire in half. Bend it like this:

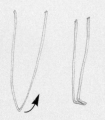

2 Peel back the top foam layer of the flip-flop and poke the ends of the wire through.

3 Put a little glue on the bent end of the wire. Re-glue the layers together.

4 Thread a couple of beads on both the wires to make the part that goes between

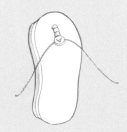

the toes. Then thread the wires through an alphabet bead in opposite directions.

5 Thread beads on each side of the wire to make straps. Bend the end of the wire to make an "L" shape. Dab a little glue on the ends of the wires and tuck them in between the foam layers.

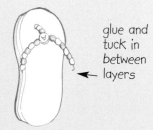

glue and tuck in between layers

For instructions on how to make criss-cross and floss straps, turn to page 112.

111

Friendship Fashions

2 Put a little glue on each end of one strip. Stick one end in between the foam layers.

3 Cross the strap over the shoe and tuck the other end in between the layers on the opposite side.

4 Do the same with the other strap, so they cross in the middle.

5 Add a dot of glue and some glitter where the straps cross, or just leave them plain.

Glue and tuck in between layers.

Criss-Cross Straps

1 Cut four thin strips of craft foam, each about 1 inch long.

Floss Straps

1 Cut four pieces of embroidery floss so they're 3 inches long each. Put all four strands together.

2 Fold a 1-inch piece of wire in half over the middle of the floss. Twist the ends of the wire together close to the floss to hold the floss in place.

3 Bend the ends of the wire in an "L" shape.

4 Peel up the top layer of foam and stick the ends of the wire

through. Dab a little glue on the ends of the wire and stick the layers back together.

5 Glue on a foam flower with tiny beads for a center.

112

trading laces

Get your friend, pull the laces out of your shoes, decorate, and swap 'em. Here are a bunch of ideas to get you going.

● **Dye the laces by soaking them in Easter-egg dye.** Make them all one color or dip in several colors.

● **Use fabric paints to make polka dots or squiggles.**

● **Write a note with a permanent marker.**

● **Use permanent markers to make rainbow stripes.**

● **Have a group of friends sign their names with a permanent marker.**

● **Sew a bead or charm in the center of the lace** (if you sew it elsewhere, it will interfere with lacing!).

● **For a splattered look, use blow pens or apply acrylic paint with a toothbrush.**

● **Tie a long piece of embroidery floss on one end of the lace.** Wrap it around the lace and tie at the other end.

● **Spread a thin layer of sparkly fabric paint on the lace and let it dry.**

113

artful key rings

My friends and I used to draw pictures of each other when we got bored in Social Studies class. I slipped one of the drawings in a clear key ring like this and started a mini-fad. Too bad the Social Studies teacher wasn't as enthusiastic about our extracurricular activities as we were. You can find clear key rings at hardware, department, and even grocery stores.

You will need:

A key ring with a clear window

A drawing or photo

Scissors

Dimensional paint

1 Trim the drawing or photo to fit in the key ring. You may have to reduce the art on a photocopy machine.

2 Slide your artwork into the key ring.

3 Decorate with dimensional paint and add beads and charms if there is a hole at the bottom.

Friendly

fun & games

fortune fun

Cheer up your friend with nothing but good fortune. Give her something to look forward to in an unusual package.

Cootie Catcher

1 Start with a square piece of paper. Fold it in the middle diagonally and then open it back up. Do the same on the other diagonal.

2 Fold all four corners into the middle.

3 Flip it over. Fold all four corners into the middle again.

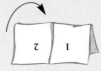

4 Write numbers 1–8 in each triangle.

5 Open each flap and write a fortune inside.

6 Flip it over and write numbers 1–4 in each square.

7 Fold the cootie catcher in half so the numbers 1–4 that you just wrote are on the outside.

8 Slide your fingers under the four corner flaps and work the creases out to make a Cootie Catcher.

Floating 8-Ball

● Insert pieces of paper that say "yes" or "no" or "maybe" into balloons. Blow them up or have them filled with helium. Hand your friend a safety pin and have her ask a question. She'll know her answer with a pop!

A Sweet Future

● Carefully unwrap a bunch of Hershey's Kisses and remove the paper tags. Replace the tags with your own personalized fortunes like "You will ace your next test" or "You will share all your candy with your BFF."

117

Friendly Fun & Games

spinner **fortune teller**

Playing with this all-purpose fortune teller is a fun party activity. And it's another great use for those free CDs that come in the mail.

You will need:

A CD that you can ruin

Two colors of paper

White paper

A pencil

Scissors

Double-stick tape

Clear contact paper

A hole punch

A lid from a plastic container like the kind used for margarine or cream cheese

A brad

1 Trace the outside of the CD on each piece of colored paper. Cut out the shapes.

2 Cut one of the circles into eight wedges, like a pie.

3 Use the double-stick tape to glue four of the wedges on the other circle.

4 Write simple answers on the white paper. Cut out and stick one on each wedge with double-stick tape.

5 Trace the CD on the contact paper. Cut out. Stick the contact paper on top of the CD, being careful not to get air bubbles.

6 Cut a spinner out of the plastic lid.

7 Punch a hole in the spinner. Attach the spinner to the middle of the CD with a brad. Now ask your friend a question and spin.

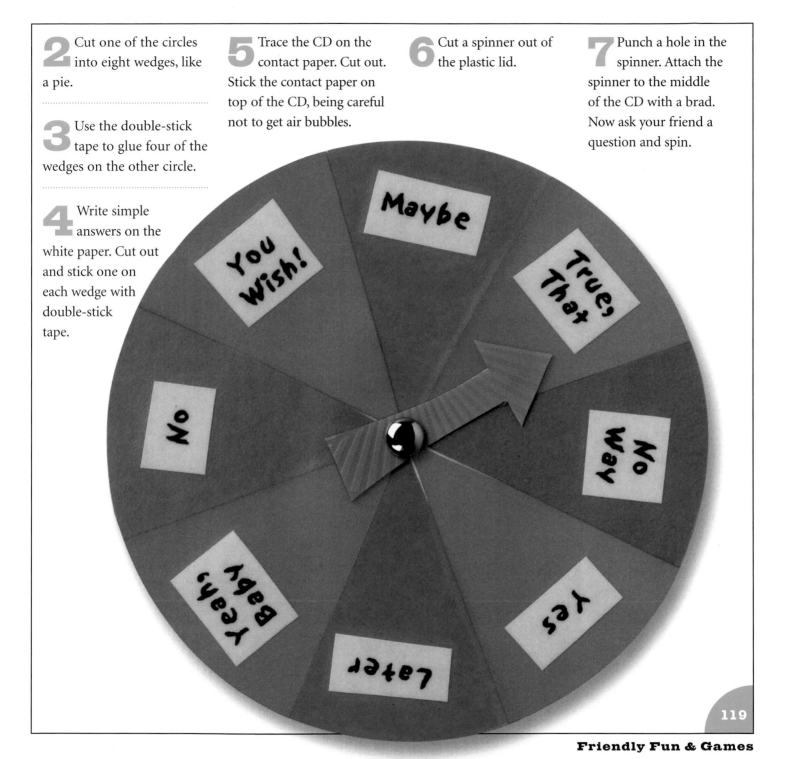

magnetic games

If you're lucky and get advertisement CDs in the mail, you can make a cool CD Friends Suncatcher (see page 16), and then use the metal container your CD came in to make this take-anywhere game tin.

You will need:

A CD tin (or use a large, flat, empty candy tin if you don't have a CD tin)

Colored paper

Pencil

Scissors

Double-stick tape

Glue

Magnetic sheets or magnetic business cards (another freebie!)

1 Trace around the tin three times on the colored paper. Cut out the shape just inside the lines.

2 Use double-stick tape to attach the paper to the insides of the tin. Attach the last piece to the top of the lid.

3 Cut four skinny strips of paper to make a tic-tac-toe board and glue down on one half of the tin. You can also just draw a tic-tac-toe board.

4 On the other half of the tin, draw or make a checkerboard. Checkerboards are eight squares by eight squares. (I made one on my paint program on my computer.) You can also cut out squares of paper and glue them down to make the board.

5 For game pieces, draw small graphics, cut them out from magazines, or print a bunch out from the computer. Use double-stick tape to attach them to the magnetic sheet. Cut them out. I used cats and dogs. My friend Pam is a dog person and I'm a cat person, so this is perfect for us.

6 Decorate the lid. I blew up the graphics from the game pieces and framed them with felt.

Design tip: Don't go with boring black and red. Try patterns and unusual colors. Do use two contrasting colors for the squares, though, so it doesn't all blur together. —♥ *Laura*

loser takes all

Try a fun variation called Loser Checkers: This time, the loser wins. Play checkers as usual, but the point of the game is that you want the other player to capture all your pieces first.

This idea works with other games, too. You can turn a game of Concentration into Reverse Concentration by trying to make as few matches as possible. One rule: You can't turn over the same two cards within three turns. The person with the most matches at the end of the game loses.

Then there's Tic-Tac-No! This time you play Tic-Tac-Toe, but DO NOT get three Xs or Os in a row, or you lose.

Friendly Fun & Games

collage trading cards

Artist Trading Cards (ATCs) are all the rage among artists who like to share their work with other artists. The idea is small original works of art that can be traded and collected. The cards are all the same size so they are easy to store and display. You can do the same thing with your friends, even if you can't draw or paint, with collage trading cards.

You will need:

An old deck of cards (You probably have one lying around the house that is useless because the cat chewed up the queen of diamonds.)

Cardstock

A pencil

Old magazines and catalogs you can cut up

Scissors

Glue stick

1 Trace around a card onto the cardstock. Cut out. Glue the card to the back of the cardstock, or cut a piece of cardstock 2½ inches x 3½ inches.

trace this card

2 Cut out images, words, and letters from the magazines and catalogs.

3 Lay out your collage on the card, then glue everything down with the glue stick (be sure to glue it really well!).

4 Write your name on the back of the card.

Best Friends Forever

Most artists trade only original artwork, but I think it's perfectly fine to photocopy your cards. Cut out the photocopies and glue cards to the backs so they are sturdy. That way you have lots for trading and one for everyone who wants one. —♥ Laura

Be somebody.

apply

Friendship Mix

When you're going to get together with a big group of your friends, be sure to take lots of pictures, and be sure to bring lots of snacks.

Here's something that everyone always loves: Tell your friends you are going to make Friendship Mix, and they should bring their favorite dry munchie snack to contribute. (Think things like M&M's, raisins, cereal, peanuts, coconut, pretzels, cheese puffs . . .) Pour everything into a great big bowl and mix it together. It's always interesting, makes for good conversation, and is sometimes really yummy! (And if you hate raisins, like some of my friends, just be polite and pick around them.)

club
us

My friends and I get together once a month to swap Artist Trading Cards and share ideas. We also have a book club, where we discuss a book we're all reading and eat bags and bags of Doritos.

A relative of mine loves Japanese manga books like *Sailor Moon*. Her manga-obsessed friends get together and swap copies so they don't have to buy them all. They also draw manga together and make T-shirts for each other with their favorite characters.

You might consider forming a club like this for you and your friends. You might want to try a Do-It-Yourself club: You get together once a month and do a craft together, share tips, and swap ideas from books and magazines.

sleepover bag & tank

This is a terrific project for a sleepover with one friend, but even better if you use it for an excuse to have a big DIY sleepover. Have everyone bring a plain pillowcase, a tank top, and fabric blowpens, if they have some. The more the merrier, and you will have lots of colors to share.

You will each need:

A pillowcase

Newspaper

A tank top

Fabric blowpens or fabric paint

1 Lay the newspaper down on the floor. Smooth the pillowcase on top of the newspaper, making sure there is paper around all the edges sticking out at least a foot.

2 Lay the tank down on the pillowcase. Smooth out.

3 Use the blowpens to make spirals of different colors and sizes all over the pillowcase and tank. If you've got a group of people, be germ-free and have each person use only one blowpen on all the pillowcases and shirts. It'll be a true group effort.

4 When you are done, let the ink dry. Remove the tank top from the pillowcase.

5 With a dark blowpen, fabric paint, or a permanent marker, write names or words on the tank, then on the white space the tank left on the pillowcase.

6 Wear the shirts for sleeping and use the pillowcase for schlepping around your stuff.

dippin' *treats*

The all-time best sleepover party treat? Peanut butter–chocolate fondue. It's easy, but get parental permission and help.

In a microwave-safe bowl, combine 1 cup of semisweet chocolate chips, ¾ cup of chunky peanut butter, 2 tablespoons of butter, and 2 tablespoons of sour cream. Microwave for 30 seconds. Take it out and stir it. Use a hot pad, because the bowl might get hot. Microwave another 30 seconds. Stir it again. If it's not melted yet, microwave it another 20 seconds and stir. It's easy to scorch chocolate chips in the microwave, so be sure to take it out when the chips are just barely melted. Dip in chocolate and vanilla wafers, angel food cake, marshmallows, and fruit.

fun things to do

Make trading cards with the pictures. Then trade 'em.

White out your hair, your smile, your eyes, or anything else you don't like about your picture. Then draw on new and improved versions!

You look *mah*-velous!

Ho, ho, ho!

If it's that bad, use a piece of paper sack to become the Unknown Student.

Best Friends Forever

A few accessories should do the trick.

A new 'do.

with school photos

Glue googly eyes on yourself.

Cool shades.

The true you.

Who are you calling Bozo?

Look at me, Ma!

Trick or treat!

april fooling

There's no harm in a little prank between friends, especially on April Fool's Day. Here are some non-embarrassing, non-dangerous, non-property-damaging gags to try if your friend has a funny bone. My friends have funny bones, but they didn't like it when I filled their sleeping bags with powdered sugar at a sleepover and they woke up glazed in the morning. So don't do anything like that. Trust me.

Sick Milk

Send your friend on an errand in the lunchroom that will take a minute or two. Meanwhile, carefully open her milk carton and add a drop of green food coloring. Close the top back up with double-sided tape. Shake it up to mix in the coloring. Then try to keep a straight face when she comes back.

Sponge Cake

Frost a big sponge with real icing and add some sprinkles so it looks like a real cake. Surprise your friend with this treat and ask her to cut it for you. Hee hee.

Silly Sipper

Before you serve the Sponge Cake, you might want to offer your friend a "beverage." Prepare some gelatin dessert ahead of time with parental help. Pour gelatin into plastic glasses and stick in a straw when it starts to gel. Store in the refrigerator until it's time to serve.

Never-Ending Muzak

Buy one of those greeting cards that plays music when you open it. Remove the chip and plant it in your friend's locker, backpack, or jacket pocket when she's not looking. Hide it as well as you can. The chip should play for about 24 hours before it runs out, and it should be about 24 months before she gets that tune out of her head.

Joke's on Me

This trick will drive your friends crazy (which is the point, isn't it?). Take a washable marker and make an obvious mark on your face. All day long, your friends will say, "Hey, you have a mark on your face!" and you will say, "Ha, ha, very funny. You think I'm going to fall for that old trick on April Fool's Day?" Then they'll say something like, "No, really, it's right there!" and you'll say, "What kind of a fool do you think I am?" This will go back and forth until they give up in exasperation. Little do they know, the joke's on them!

pencil games

Here are a few games to play with a pencil and paper if you have some time to kill with a friend.

Pipes

Draw a board that looks like this, using two colors of pencil or pen:

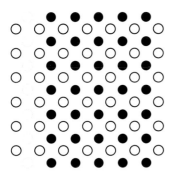

Players take turns connecting two dots together. The object is to draw a connected line from one side of the board to the other, using only your color dots, and without crossing any lines or skipping around (you can only draw a continuous line). You want to prevent your friend from doing the same.

CrossGrid

Each player draws a grid, four squares by four squares. Take turns calling out a letter—any letter. Players can put the letter anywhere on the grid they choose. The object is to spell words crossword style, across or down. When all the squares are filled, keep score. Four-letter words are worth ten points and three-letter words are worth five points. No points for two-letter words. Play to fifty or one hundred points.

If / Then Game

This is my favorite game, but you need at least three people to play. Each player has two pieces of paper. On one, you write the first part of a sentence, beginning with "If." For example, "If Rachel got a cat." Finish the sentence on the other piece of paper, beginning with "then." For example, "then she would have to buy kitty litter." Another example: "If Michelle got a bad haircut," "then we'd have to fix it for her." Everybody mixes up the IFs in one pile and the THENs in another pile. Take turns grabbing one paper from each pile and reading the result. "If Rachel got a cat," "then we'd have to fix it for her" and "If Michelle got a bad haircut," "then she would have to buy kitty litter."

Sort-of bingo

Bingo cards are great for long road trips or even as a party activity. Ask your friends to help you make them, because that's half (or more!) of the fun. The idea is to use everyday objects that people can spot. Pam once put a picture of John Travolta on one square, and a sea slug on another. We did live near the ocean, but the chances of winning with one of those cards were pretty slim.

You will need:

Old Bingo cards or cardstock

Scissors

Magazines and catalogs you can cut up or paper and pens to draw with

Glue stick

1 If you don't have Bingo cards to use, draw a 5" x 5" grid on the cardstock. Label the middle square FREE.

2 Cut out pictures of everyday objects to fit inside the Bingo squares and glue them in place with the glue stick. Or you could draw the pictures yourself.

3 Photocopy the cards so you have a bunch of each one.

4 To play, all you have to do is cross out the things you see. You win if you get a row up, down, or diagonally. (You don't use the Bingo letters, which is why this is called Sort-of Bingo.) You can also play Blackout, which you win if you spot everything on your card—but that's only for a really long trip. It's harder than it might seem to spot a sea slug.

132

Two-of-a-Kind

Kind

jewelry

friendship stack rings

These are easy and cheap to make, so stack 'em up! If you've got lots of friends, you'll have to grow longer fingers.

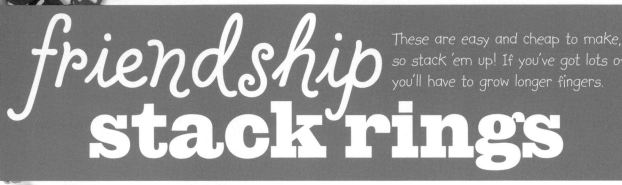

You will need:

- **24- or 26-gauge wire**
- **Alphabet beads**
- **Small beads**
- **Fingernail clippers**

1 Using the fingernail clippers, clip off a piece of wire about 12 inches long.

2 Thread on an alphabet bead.

3 Thread the smaller beads on each side of the alphabet bead until the ring is big enough to fit snugly around your finger.

4 Thread one more bead on one end of the wire. Thread the other end of the wire through the bead in the opposite direction.

5 Pull on the wires to form the ring. Tightly wrap each end of the wire a few times around the main wire, right up next to the last bead.

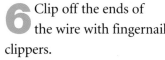

clip wire

6 Clip off the ends of the wire with fingernail clippers.

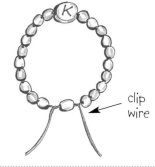

There are lots of ways to make stack rings. Try some of these, then invent your own. — ♥ *Laura*

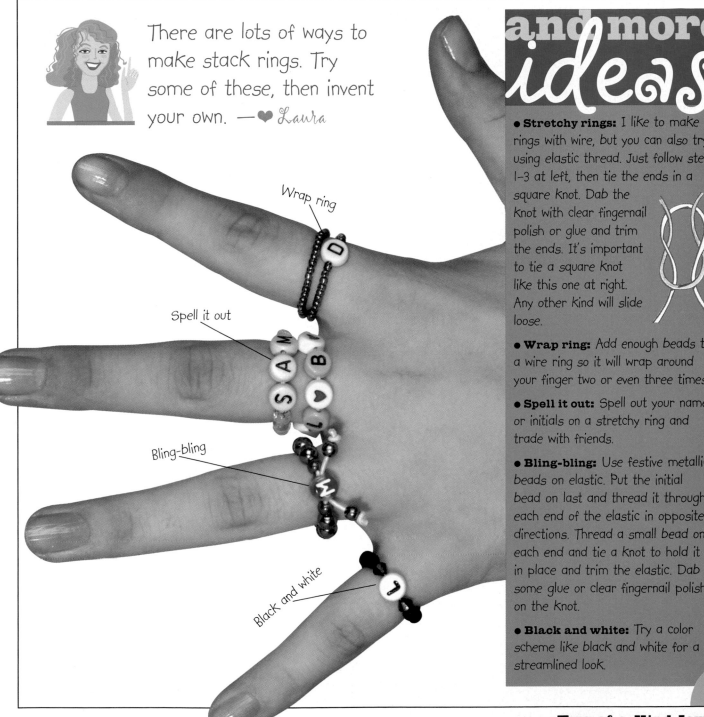

Wrap ring

Spell it out

Bling-bling

Black and white

and more ideas

● **Stretchy rings:** I like to make rings with wire, but you can also try using elastic thread. Just follow steps 1–3 at left, then tie the ends in a square knot. Dab the knot with clear fingernail polish or glue and trim the ends. It's important to tie a square knot like this one at right. Any other kind will slide loose.

● **Wrap ring:** Add enough beads to a wire ring so it will wrap around your finger two or even three times.

● **Spell it out:** Spell out your name or initials on a stretchy ring and trade with friends.

● **Bling-bling:** Use festive metallic beads on elastic. Put the initial bead on last and thread it through each end of the elastic in opposite directions. Thread a small bead on each end and tie a knot to hold it in place and trim the elastic. Dab some glue or clear fingernail polish on the knot.

● **Black and white:** Try a color scheme like black and white for a streamlined look.

135

braided friendship bracelets

You don't have to know a fancy knotting technique to make friendship bracelets. These are the easiest friendship bracelets in the world, they look good, and you can make them out of almost any kind of cord.

You will need:

Cord (embroidery floss, plastic lace, leather cord)

Scissors

A friend

1 Cut two strands of cord. One should be 2 feet long and one should be 1 foot long.

2 Fold the long strand in half. Hold the second piece together with the folded end and tie a knot, leaving a small loop at the top.

3 Have your friend hold this end of the cord to keep the whole thing taut while you braid.

4 When the braid is long enough to just fit around your friend's wrist, tie the strands in a knot.

5 Wrap the bracelet around your friend's wrist and tie the loose strands through the loop. Trim the ends.

Tips!

● **Add beads randomly while braiding.**

● **If you're using thin cord, make a double-wrap bracelet.**

136

Tie them around a ponytail.

Use them to tie things onto your backpack, or just to decorate it.

use your bracelets

You can use friendship bracelets for all sorts of things besides bracelets.

Thread them through the spiral of a notebook.

Use two to tie up your sleeves.

Tie them on your belt loops.

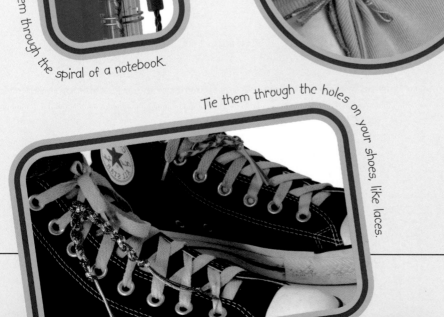

Tie them through the holes on your shoes, like laces.

Two-of-a-Kind Jewelry

leather charm
necklaces

Easy and cute.
Enough said.

You will need:

Suede or leather cord
(Buy it by the yard at a fabric store.)

Charm

Beads

Scissors

Jump ring (or wire to make your own)

1 Cut a piece of cord as long as you want your necklace to be (don't forget to include enough cord to tie a knot at the back).

2 Put a jump ring on the charm. Thread the cord through the jump ring and center the charm. If you don't have a jump ring, make one by wrapping a piece of wire twice around the end of a thin crochet needle or other long round thing. I used the non-sticky end of my sucker stick once and it worked like a charm (ha!).

3 Add beads to each side of the cord. That's it!

138

Try these variations:

● After you put on the charm, thread both ends of the cord through a large bead. Separate the cord and then put a few beads on each side.

● Thread a piece of wire through the jump ring or charm. Thread beads on both ends of the wire. Loop the ends of the wire over the middle of the cord twice and trim the ends.

● **Letter charms:** Thread a few beads on a wire to make a circle. Leave some slack in the wire so there is room for the beads to move around. Have each of your friends make a charm out of wire, beads, and letter beads with their initials.

Hook the charms onto the bead and wire circle so they dangle from the bottom. Thread the circle onto a piece of leather, or tie the middle of the cord onto the circle.

● **Hinge book:** Use a tiny hinge (you can get it from a hardware store) instead of a regular charm. Thread the jump ring through a hole near the top of the hinge. Cover the front of the hinge with paper (double-stick tape or white glue both work fine) and decorate. On the inside, glue a tiny picture, poem, or note.

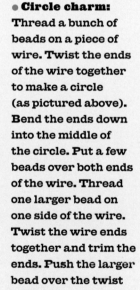

● **Circle charm:** Thread a bunch of beads on a piece of wire. Twist the ends of the wire together to make a circle (as pictured above). Bend the ends down into the middle of the circle. Put a few beads over both ends of the wire. Thread one larger bead on one side of the wire. Twist the wire ends together and trim the ends. Push the larger bead over the twist to hide it.

● **Earrings:** Hook the letter charms onto earring hooks. Each of you can make a pair with your initials, and then swap one.

Two-of-a-Kind Jewelry

This is an oldie but a goodie, with a brand-new twist. Before you make the beads, write good wishes for each other on the inside of the strips of paper. After the beads are rolled, you can wear the good karma everywhere.

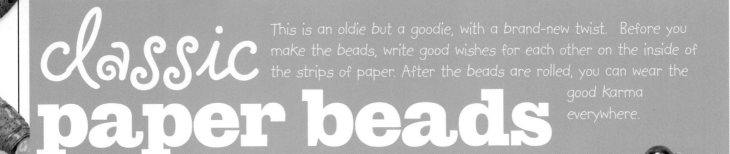

You will need:

Paper that's at least 8 inches long (wrapping paper, magazine pages, pages from old books, notes from friends, scrapbook paper, origami paper, junk mail . . .)

¼-inch-wide beads

Scissors

A toothpick, lollipop stick, or bamboo skewer

Glue stick

1 Cut a strip of paper about ¾ of an inch wide, and about 8–12 inches long. Cut one end of the strip into a point.

2 Write your good wishes on the back side of the paper strip.

3 With the non-pointed end of the paper, start rolling the strip around the toothpick, being careful to keep the paper centered. When there is about 1 inch left to roll, apply the glue stick to the back side and continue rolling so the bead sticks together.

Variations:

● **Try different widths of paper and different materials. You'll be surprised at the variety you can make.**

● **String your beads on elastic, beading string, leather cord, or ribbon. Try stringing them with regular beads and charms.**

page from a book

magazine ad

note from a friend

scrapbook paper

origami paper

clay beads

Try these super-easy swirl beads from air-dry clay to make friendship chokers or anklets (see page 148).

shaped beads

shaped beads

cinnamon-roll beads

shaped beads

shaped beads

polka-dot beads

1 Roll two long skinny snakes of contrasting air-dry clay colors.

2 Twist the snakes together like a candy cane.

3 Mush up the clay until it has a nice swirly pattern. Don't mush too much, or the colors will blend and look pukey. Roll the whole thing into a log. Cut ¾-inch beads off the log.

4 Use something poky, like a crochet needle or a barbeque skewer, to make a hole in the middle of the bead. Thread the bead on a piece of leather and let it dry (usually overnight).

5 Tie a knot on each side of the bead or add a pony bead on each side. Done!

141

hookless crochet jewelry

You don't need a crochet hook to make crocheted rings, bracelets, or chokers. All you need is your finger. Pam and I used to make these on the bus ride to school. By the end of the year, almost everyone on the bus had one tied on a wrist or backpack.

You will need:

Craft floss (Try yarn and other interesting fibers, too.)

Scissors

1 Wrap the end of the yarn twice around the pointer finger of your left hand (if you're right-handed—reverse if you're a leftie).

2 Pick up the back loop and pull it over the first loop and off your finger.

3 Tighten the strings a little. Be careful to keep everything in place until you form a knot with the next stitch.

4 Wrap a new loop in front of the old loop. Repeat the process and keep going until it is as long as you would like.

5 Cut off the yarn, thread the end through the last loop and pull snug. Done!

Add a Bead

Crochet until you are about halfway done. Cut the floss so it's as long as you think you will need for the rest of the chain. Slide a bead on. Continue crocheting around the bead.

the hands have it

If you've got an out-there style, be bold with your friends and wear this unusual hand jewelry.

You will need:

Beading elastic (thin and round)

Scissors

A variety of beads

Glue

1 Cut a piece of elastic so it's about 2 feet long. String enough beads onto the middle of the cord to make a ring around your middle finger.

2 Center the beads on the elastic. Thread both ends of the elastic through one larger bead, in the opposite directions, to make the ring.

3 Thread some smaller beads on each strand of elastic. Thread both ends of the elastic through one larger bead, in opposite directions, to make a loop. Make two or three loops until the beaded elastic almost reaches your wrist.

4 String enough beads on each side of the elastic to fit around your wrist. Tie the elastic and trim the ends. Put a dab of glue on the knot to secure it.

143

Two-of-a-Kind Jewelry

riveting **friendship bracelets**

Say it with brads. Spell out any message that you want with these easy, fun friendship bracelets.

1 Cut a strip of craft foam about ½ inch wide, and long enough to fit around your friend's wrist, plus 1 inch.

2 Stick the brads through the foam and open them up. Leave about ½ inch on each end brad-free.

3 Write letters on the brads with the permanent marker.

4 Wrap the bracelet around your friend's wrist. Overlap the ends and stick a brad through both layers of foam to hold the bracelet in place.

You will need:

Craft foam

Brads (The scrapbook section of the craft store has neat mini-brads and different shapes, but regular brads work fine, too.)

Scissors

Permanent marker

Secret Message Bracelets

I used to make these secret message bracelets for my friends who were boys. They wouldn't wear any other type of jewelry, but rubber bands were macho enough. (Until I wrote "Kiss Me" on one. Then even these bracelets had cooties, apparently.)

Stretch a thick rubber band around a big book or a metal lunch box, or the back of a straight-back chair. It needs to be good and stretched out. Write a message on it with a permanent marker. Let it dry, then let it snap back to its original shape. You can't tell what it says until you stretch it out again. Try writing funny jokes on the bracelets for non-cootie fun. Here are a few favorites:

Where do you find a dog with no legs?

Right where you left him.

If you're an American outside the restroom, what are you inside the restroom?

European.

What did the frog order at the fast-food restaurant?

French Flies and a Diet Croke.

Where did the king keep his armies?

Up his sleevies.

What did the alien say when it landed in a garden?

Take me to your weeder!

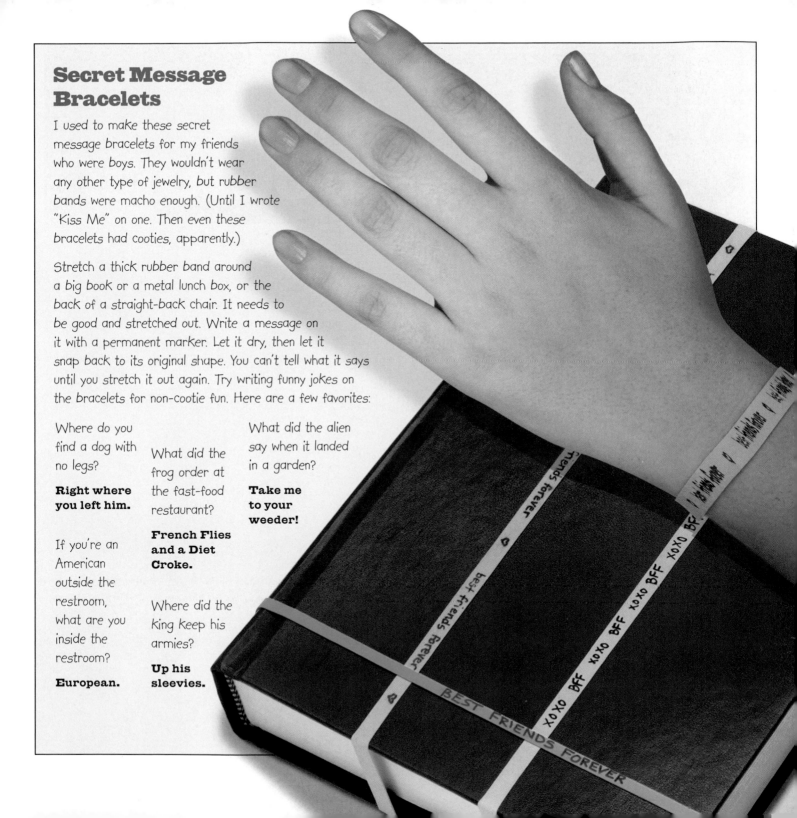

swapping charms

If you have a normal charm bracelet, you know that once you put a charm on, it stays put. It takes a lot of effort to take it off or switch it. But you can make charms that open and close easily, and you can switch them around all you want. This makes for perfect friendship crafting—you can make bunches of charms and swap them with friends.

You will need:

A charm

A jump ring

A lobster-claw clasp

A bracelet

1 Attach a jump ring to your charm. You do this by threading it on just like a key on a key chain.

2 Attach a lobster-claw clasp to the jump ring.

3 Open the clasp and attach it to any bracelet. Take it off just as easily!

Charms

Puzzle Pieces: Coat a puzzle piece with Mod Podge or white glue. Put a piece of tissue paper on the top. Spread on another coat of Mod Podge and sprinkle glitter on top. Let dry. Trim or tear off the excess tissue paper. Poke a hole in the top of the piece with a darning needle or small nail.

Beads: Thread a piece of wire through a large bead, so there is about an inch of wire sticking out the bottom of the bead. Thread a smaller bead on the tail of the wire. Roll up the wire around the smaller bead to hold everything in place. Make a loop at the top of the bead, wrap the end around the wire close to the bead to secure it, and trim with fingernail clippers.

Bottle Caps: Paint a design on the back of a bottle cap. (Or follow the directions on page 78 for bottle-cap magnets, but leave off the magnet.) Make a hole in the top with a small nail. If the jump ring is too small to fit through the hole, loop wire through the bottle cap and attach the ring to the loop.

Shrink Art: Probably the most fun way to make charms. Follow the package directions. Be sure to punch a hole in the top of the charms with a hole punch before you bake them.

Two-of-a-Kind Jewelry

cool anklets

Sometimes the simplest is the best.

1 Cut 2 pieces of suede cord to fit around your ankles, plus 3 inches.

2 Thread on alphabet beads and tie knots to keep them in place.

3 Tie loosely around your ankle.

You and your BFF make a great pair whether you are crafting together or just hanging out. Caring and sharing is what makes your friendship special. —♥ *Laura*